The Best
Start in Life

PROFESSOR DAVID BARKER

The Best Start in Life

How a woman's diet can protect her child from disease in later life

CENTURY

Published by Century Books in 2003

1 3 5 7 9 10 8 6 4 2

First published in the United Kingdom in 2003 by Century

Century
The Random House Group Limited
20 Vauxhall Bridge Road, London, SW1V 2SA

Random House Australia (Pty) Limited
20 Alfred Street, Milsons Point, Sydney,
New South Wales 2061, Australia

Random House New Zealand Limited
18 Poland Road, Glenfield
Auckland 10, New Zealand

Random House (Pty) Limited
Endulini, 5a Jubilee Road, Parktown 2193, South Africa

The Random House Group Limited Reg. No. 954009

www.randomhouse.co.uk

A CIP catalogue record for this book
is available from the British Library

Papers used by Random House
are natural, recyclable products made from wood grown in
sustainable forests. The manufacturing processes conform to
the environmental regulations of the country of origin

ISBN 1 8441 3152 1

Printed and bound in Great Britain by
Mackays of Chatham PLC, Chatham, Kent

CONTENTS

Man brings all that he has or can have into the world with him.
Man is born like a garden ready planted and sown

(William Blake 1757–1827)

ACKNOWLEDGEMENTS

This book describes a baby's journey. It also describes a scientific journey, one which revealed for the first time that good nutrition in the womb and in the early years after birth may protect against heart disease, diabetes and stroke in later life. This journey was made with colleagues at the University of Southampton, and in the company of doctors, scientists and nurses elsewhere in Britain, in other European countries, in the USA, India and China. But for their discoveries this book could not have been written.

The photographs of refrigerators inside the cover come from a study of the contents of ordinary household fridges in the homes of young women in an English city. The photos were taken by Magda Segal and provide startling evidence of the paucity of fresh foods in the diets of many young people in Western countries. Charts 2 and 3 are published with permission from the Child Growth Foundation.

It is a pleasure to acknowledge the help of my friend and colleague, Dr Sian Robinson. She has given me expert advice on nutrition and, using her own experience as a mother, has helped to write simple guidelines within which each mother can choose the foods that are best suited to herself and her baby.

FOREWORD

Future parents want the best for their children, wishing them to be born healthy and to live long lives free of avoidable illness. However, the twentieth century saw an explosion of coronary heart disease, which accounts for one in four deaths among men and one in six among women. Researchers have identified several factors that can increase an individual's risk of developing coronary heart disease, particularly at a young age, and these include raised blood pressure, smoking, physical inactivity, poor diet and obesity. In addition, the disease is more common in some families than in others due to a combination of inherited and environmental factors.

Nevertheless, doctors looking after patients who develop a heart attack or who live with angina have seen many who lack any of these identifiable risk factors. This led Professor David Barker and colleagues to investigate other causes of premature coronary heart disease, especially those occurring in northern parts of the United Kingdom where the disease is unusually common. They noted that rates of heart disease were predicted by the proportion of babies who had died before the age of one year in the 1920s. Babies who died in the first month were small, because their mothers were undernourished, whilst those surviving beyond one month only to die before the age of one year did so because of poor conditions in the world into which they had been born. These included poor housing, crowding and inadequate feeding, which clearly reflect the environment.

In the first few chapters of his book, Professor Barker explores links with the Industrial Revolution, the 'dark satanic mills' of Northern England, the migration of country dwellers into London and the effects of civil war in the United States of America. The team searched for archives, not only in England, but also Finland, and identified important records in Hertfordshire, Preston,

Sheffield and Helsinki. The detailed information contained in these records confirmed the importance of a mother's health and nutrition during pregnancy (and earlier), which sets the scene for long-term health and the well-being of her offspring. Equally, infant nutrition – especially breastfeeding – has important consequences for health in adult life.

This fascinating detective work is complemented by knowledge gained from animals – bees and caddis flies, lizards, birds, and mammals, both wild and domesticated – which proves that it is the mother and her nutrition who control the growth of her child in the womb. For small offspring, 'catch-up' growth can be important as long as it is completed by twelve months after birth, emphasising the importance of infant feeding practices and weaning. Collectively, these critical periods of development, both within the womb and in the first three years after birth, set the scene for either the development or avoidance of coronary heart disease, high blood pressure, diabetes and the likelihood of stroke. The message to women is clear-cut: if you want your baby to grow up healthy, then as a future mother you must look after yourself before and during pregnancy, and pay attention not only to your diet, but also to that of your newborn child. Professor Barker provides clear evidence from dietary histories obtained from young women that many do not take a balanced diet, and although there are impediments to achieving one, he offers solutions as well as important advice on infant nutrition and weaning.

The British Heart Foundation has been delighted to support some of the pivotal research which put the early origins of adult disease concept on the map. We continue to support Professor Barker and his colleagues in studies based in India, Finland and his home city of Southampton.

Professor Sir Charles George
Medical Director, British Heart Foundation
January 2003

INTRODUCTION

Our understanding of the best diet for a pregnant woman was born out of calamity. Throughout Europe one hundred years ago thousands of babies died every week. Some died while they were in the womb, while others died in the days after birth – died because they were small and puny and lacked the vitality to meet the challenge of doing for themselves functions that their mothers had hitherto performed for them: eating, breathing and excreting waste. 'Hereditarians', people who believe that the course of life is ordained by genes acquired at conception, argued that these dead babies were a normal part of nature, the weeding out of people of 'inferior stock' before they in turn could reproduce and, by passing their defective genes on to the next generation, weaken the nation's genetic stock. But to the doctors and midwives who cared for pregnant women at the time, another process was obviously responsible. The mothers were undernourished. Many more newborn babies died in places where people lived in the worst conditions: on the poorest agricultural land where food was scarce, and in the slums of the towns which sprang up as the Industrial Revolution burgeoned. The mothers of the dead babies were thin because they did not have sufficient food, and were stunted because they had grown up in want of the foods that allow children to grow. The stores of food in their bodies were insufficient to nourish their babies through the pregnancy, and whatever food they ate during pregnancy was mostly used to meet the demands of their long hours of manual work in fields and factories.

Around the beginning of the twentieth century improving economic conditions lowered the price of food and European governments began to take an interest in pregnancy because the falling numbers of births of healthy, live-born baby boys threatened their ability to raise armies and defend their territories.

Midwifery services were established. Yet the sight of starving pregnant women remained commonplace and, because their condition was most pitiable as they approached delivery, charitable organisations that provided food focused on women in late pregnancy.

Then the science of nutrition began to advance. An early success was the discovery that rickets could be prevented by better food. This terrible disease affected infants, especially those in some of the great European cities of which Glasgow and Vienna were world centres, though for different reasons. When an infant develops rickets its bones soften; as it toddles the leg bones bend under the stress and the pelvis deforms. These are permanent changes. As the child grows and is better fed its bones strengthen, but the deformity persists: the boy becomes a man unfit for manual work and, far worse, the girl becomes a woman unable to give birth to her baby, which becomes lodged between the deformed bones that border the birth canal. Both mother and baby may die. The discovery that this disease was due to lack of Vitamin D pointed to the potency of single nutrients in causing common disorders and established a way of thinking about the diets of mothers and babies that focused on individual nutrients, and has persisted until this day. As a result, instead of studying the variety and balance of foods, we continue to search for 'magic bullets', supplements of single nutrients – vitamins and minerals – that can be taken by a mother to serve like an ancient charm to ward off disaster. The link between Vitamin D and rickets also showed that deficiencies in the diets of babies and infants can lead to life-long changes in the structure of the body – a major theme of this book.

In Western countries food is now plentiful and, happily, disaster – death or deformity – is rare. In Britain we are now debating whether to change the diets of 50 million people by adding folic acid to their bread in the hope of preventing 400 disasters – babies with spina bifida – per year. But the aim of a good diet during pregnancy extends far beyond the avoidance of disaster. After our children are born we encourage the development of their minds, we play with them, take them to places, socialise them. Our purpose is not merely to avoid disaster – mental incapacity – rather we have aspirations to give them a wide experience so that as adults they meet the challenges of the world outside. We accept that the results of our endeavours are largely outside our control, that each child in a family responds differently. We do not know whether this is through inheritance or the different experiences of children even within the same family, but we accept that our children's development is governed by natural processes we can enable and assist, but not control. These natural processes and their variation between one child and another are readily apparent even during infancy, the first year after birth, but they begin at conception.

The brain continues to develop after birth. So, too, does the immune system through which we meet the challenge of infection. As a child grows it requires experience of the world to develop its bodily systems. These systems, which include those through which we handle our food – breaking it down, using it for energy or storing it – need to be stimulated before they can function. A kitten's eyes open ten days after birth. If one of the eyes is held closed again for only a day or so when it is around four weeks old the eye will be blind forever. Without appropriate experience at a critical stage of development the eye does not learn how to see. Once it has learned it is no longer vulnerable. Even if a kitten's eyes are held closed for many days when it is three months old there is no lasting effect.

Unlike the brain and the immune system, most systems of the body are established and largely completed before birth. The environmental stimuli come from the mother. In the womb the baby develops its own unique 'internal environment', regulated by the brain and controlled by hormonal messengers. We try to keep this environment within ourselves constant through our lives in the face of whatever challenges the external environment poses. This is the basis of good health. Our physical responses – to food, stress, the opposite sex – are determined by our internal environments. This book describes recent research funded by the Medical Research Council, the British Heart Foundation and other medical research organisations, which has shown that coronary heart disease, diabetes, stroke and other diseases of later life have their origins in the internal environment created in the womb.

The creation of the internal environment begins at an early stage, in the embryo. For a century the general view has been that, because a baby is small in early pregnancy and therefore needs only small amounts of food, it obtains everything it needs. We overlooked the fact that nutrition can affect the embryo through the powerful hormonal and other signals it evokes in the mother. These signals begin to set the internal environment, giving the embryo experiences which mould it for the future. If during the past century doctors and scientists had looked beyond the starving mothers among the peasantry and slum-dwellers of Europe, and taken counsel from the natural world around them, the importance of the mother's food stores and fitness at the time of conception would have been obvious. But we have lost touch with the natural world, with our close affinity to other animals.

From infancy we offer our children rich and varied experiences of the world outside the home, and through these their responses and behaviours are moulded and established for a lifetime. Similarly, life in the womb is a time of moulding, being shaped by experience, and no experience is more important than the food which passes from mother to baby. A varied and balanced diet shapes the baby's organs and systems in ways that prepare it for a long and healthy life. It is not the acquisition of genes at conception that determine them, as modern-day hereditarians would have us believe. Rather it is the interplay between the genes and the environment during development. The queen bee and the worker bee have the same genes: they differ because of the different food they were given as they developed.

I

Heart attacks begin in the womb

HEART ATTACK

He turns into Branch Road and walks down the hill towards the embankment. On either side long rows of terraced houses, grey and cream, end at the high bank which carries the Leeds-to-Liverpool canal through the town. Beyond the canal, factory chimneys are silhouetted against the hills, green on their lower slopes, brown from the moorlands above. Their chimneys no longer smoke, for cotton weaving has ceased in Burnley. The cotton industry enriched an empire but condemned generations of Burnley people to long hours in the mills and to poor, crowded housing built around the mills on land too marshy to be farmed. The moist air in this damp valley was ideal for weaving.

John Clegg continues down the hill. Each house is the same, a door into the single front room on the ground floor, a bedroom above, two other rooms at the back. Halfway down the hill he stops to buy the *Evening Telegraph*. The bald man behind the counter says nothing, merely nods, even though he and John are cousins. John's cousin is known as a man of few words, a man to be avoided at family funerals and weddings. Leaving the shop, John looks at the sky and rehearses the choice he makes each day. He has had his evening meal before he left home. Should he now walk back up the hill and have a pint of beer in the Royal Butterfly on his way home, on the other side of the railway line, or should he continue his walk down the hill to the canal embankment and along to the town football ground? Spending the days driving his truck, he likes a walk in the evening as it helps to keep the weight down.

Though the wind is cold, and dark clouds fly across Pendle Hill, he walks on down Branch Road. At the embankment he turns, passing Dean Mill which, abandoned by the weavers, is now occupied by light industry and Asian businesses. Rain is falling. He quickens his pace and begins to walk back up the hill. The pain is sudden and severe; across the front of his chest, down his left arm, up into his neck. He feels his heart beating, fast but without force, fluttering. He is dizzy. He falls to his knees. His head touches the ground and he rolls on to his side.

He is in an ambulance. The pain continues. He cannot breathe. He is lifted on to a trolley and wheeled along corridors. People stand over him, but his eyes do not focus. Will someone find his wife? 'Mr Clegg, you have had a heart attack,' the young doctor tells him. 'You will need to stay with us.' He is in a ward with other men, attached by wires to machines around their beds. Lights flash, heartbeats are registered on green lines moving continuously across glass screens.

In the morning the ward sister comes and sits down beside his bed. She explains that the arteries that supply blood to the muscle of his heart have become hardened and narrowed. The pain he experienced was the result of a blood clot suddenly forming in one of the narrowed arteries so that the muscle received too little blood and developed cramp. This, she says, is called coronary heart disease. Part of his heart muscle is now probably dead and will form a scar. After he leaves hospital it may be some while before he can resume his work as a truck driver lest he has another attack while driving.

'Sister, why did this happen to me? I have always been healthy. I don't smoke – although I am a little overweight, I am nothing like as fat as many of my friends.'

'The doctor's notes say that your father had heart disease, Mr Clegg, so it runs in the family. It's in your genes. Heart disease is common in people who live around here.'

'That's more or less what she said to me,' said Mohan Rao, an Indian man in the bed next door, who had heard the conversation. 'Except that she said it's my Indian genes, which make me prone to diabetes. A lot of people in Mysore, where I come from, have diabetes and it leads to heart disease. I have got both and I'm only thirty-five years old and not particularly fat.'

Some weeks after John Clegg left the hospital, feeling tired and a little weak but otherwise well, he returns to the Outpatient Clinic at Burnley General Hospital. The consultant tells him that his blood pressure is high and he will need to take tablets. The level of cholesterol in his blood is also a little high. His blood sugar levels, however, are normal and he does not have diabetes. He is sent to see a dietician, who tells him to eat less fatty foods, to eat margarine instead of butter, to eat less salt, and more fruit and vegetables. She tells him to take more exercise. In the ward he had been given a sheet of paper listing the kinds of moderate exercise that are appropriate, which include walking at a fast pace for twenty minutes each day. The paper also said that he could still make love to his wife, though 'in moderation', which confused him.

He leaves the hospital worried. At forty-five years of age he cannot afford to retire, even though his wife earns money working in a supermarket. It has settled in his mind that his heart attack was his fault, due to the way he has lived. Though he has lived in the same way and eaten the same food as many of his neighbours, with heart disease running in the family he should have been more careful. He is uncertain what he should have been careful of, but it is something to do with fried foods, fish and chips, cream, the salt pot and being a truck driver. He is glad that he does not smoke because if he did, everyone would agree that his heart attack was his own fault.

AN ORTHODOXY IS BORN

What John Clegg was told in hospital was what people with coronary heart disease, henceforward in this book to be referred to simply as heart disease, are told across the Western world. His story is one that is rehearsed every day across Europe and the US. The advice he received is not wrong, and he may prolong his life by improving his lifestyle and taking his tablets. The advice is, however, seriously incomplete. It takes no account of what each of us knows from our own observation – that the same lifestyle has different effects on different people. Some fat men who live on hamburgers and chips and smoke do not get heart disease, while others perish. To doctors who have worked in coronary care units the 'blameless' lives of many of our patients is apparent. To say that their sickness must therefore be genetic is merely to dismiss the issue. Genes are not automatic switches: whether or not they become active depends on what else is happening to the body.

The ward sister told John Clegg that heart attacks occur because the arteries in the heart muscle become hardened and narrowed. Hardening of the arteries is part of the history of mankind. It has been found in the arteries of Egyptian mummies, in the arteries of a fifty-year-old Chinese woman mummified in 1120 BC, in the arteries of a man buried in the ice on the Austrian–Italian border 5000 years ago. Until a hundred years ago, however, heart attacks were uncommon. They appeared suddenly and increased rapidly, so that fifty years later they had become the commonest cause of death in the Western world. Today there are rising epidemics in the Third World, in India, China, South America – 6 million people die from heart disease each year and half a million of those are in the USA; 150 million people in the world have diabetes. Soon these diseases will be the most common cause of death throughout the world. Something more than hardening of the arteries must be happening. What could have caused such a catastrophe?

The most obvious clue is that it is something to do with becoming richer and better nourished. A favoured explanation in the early days of the worldwide research activity which developed fifty years ago was that it was the result of eating more fat. Foods which contain fat, such as meat and butter, tend to be lacking in the diets of poorer people. They are expensive. Surprisingly, there is no precise scientific definition of the word 'fat'. It is generally applied to foods that are obviously fatty in nature, greasy in texture and do not mix with water. Chemists use the word 'lipid' to describe a much larger group of chemicals all of which have in common the property of not dissolving in water. It is convenient to use the word fat when discussing the fatty components of food, and lipids when discussing how the body handles, or 'metabolises', fats. Fats eaten in food are broken down by the body into their components and then reconstituted to form lipids such as cholesterol, which have particular functions. Cholesterol is an important part of the walls or 'membranes' that form the barrier between a cell and the world outside it. For reasons that are not well understood, cholesterol is uniquely important for animal membranes – plant membranes do not use it but contain another lipid. The cholesterol in our diet comes almost entirely from animal foods, but the body can make its own cholesterol from other sources.

Forty years ago discovery of the link between the amount of cholesterol in the blood and the risk of heart disease seemed to herald a major breakthrough that would allow us to control the epidemic. Since animal fats are the source of the cholesterol in the blood, the argument ran, and since a high blood cholesterol predisposes to heart disease, the disease would dwindle if we ate less fat. Though the first two propositions are undeniably correct, proof of the third has been elusive, despite a massive investment of research resources. A direct link between how much fat a person eats and his or her risk of heart disease has proved difficult to establish, and those of us treating patients have become increasingly frustrated by the poor results of altering people's diets in an attempt to reduce the cholesterol levels in their blood.

Nevertheless, and not unreasonably, public health programmes were launched. Older people in Wales enquired why in their youth the government had told them to drink more milk, to prevent consumption, and now in middle life they were instructed to drink less to prevent heart disease. Everywhere dairy industries were thrown into turmoil. Tony Mitchell, Professor of Medicine at the University of Nottingham, gave mocking lectures entitled 'Should every cow carry a government health warning?'.

But out of the trough of frustration came dietary fibre, borne on the wings of an old idea and fuelled by the riches of the breakfast cereal industry. In 1920 Rendle Short, Professor of Surgery at the University of Bristol, published a paper in the

British Journal of Surgery. Anecdotes reveal him as a devout man who did not want to meet his Maker without giving an account of his appreciation of the wonderful world that he had lived in. Each year he chose a topic for his close inspection. One year, during the First World War, he chose appendicitis, a disease that was rare until around 1890, but rose suddenly and steeply to become one of the most common surgical emergencies. Over a ten-year period, 5 per cent of the population in Scotland developed the disease. It killed young people, it killed the rich – what could have caused this outbreak?

In his paper, Rendle Short concluded that the disease had arisen as a result of 'the relatively less quantity of cellulose [roughage] eaten on account of the wider use of imported foods'. By eating less of the fibre in vegetables and coarse bread, people had slowed the passage of food through the bowels, leading to stasis and infection. His paper led to a leading article in the *Lancet* and to the marketing of All-Bran. However, the idea that acute appendicitis was caused by lack of fibre failed to withstand more rigorous analysis. The origins of the disease probably lie some-where in the altered responses to infection of people growing up in an increasingly more hygienic world, where the experience of infection that a child requires to establish its own immune defences is decreasing. In the 1970s, by which time appendicitis was beginning to disappear, the dietary fibre hypothesis was reincarnated as an explanation for a whole group of diseases including heart disease and diabetes. This, too, has failed to withstand closer scrutiny.

People with hypertension – high blood pressure – are at risk of heart disease and may benefit from eating less salt. If the body retains too much salt, blood pressure rises. In the short term this happens because the fluid in the blood is increased to dilute the salt; in the longer term salt makes the walls of the arteries contract so that they become narrowed. Perhaps everyone was eating too much salt? Though the extensive Inter-Salt Study of salt intake and blood pressure in fifty-two populations around the world gave only limited support to this, soon salt was only available in our hospital canteen in small individual packs to prevent us adding too much to our food – an effective strategy in that the packs are so poorly manufactured that around half of them contain no salt at all. Since most of the salt in our diets comes with the food we eat, especially processed foods – and even bread contains salt – it is merely a symbolic gesture.

Researchers examined what was known about the changes in consumption of particular foods in the nineteenth century that could have triggered the heart disease epidemic. Was it, in Britain, the increasing importation of sugar from our empire? Was it our ultimate success, after many disasters, in solving the technical problems of shipping fresh meat from the Americas? Was it a fall in fish consumption? But nothing added up.

Aspects of lifestyles other than diet were considered. Obesity and lack of exercise are clearly linked to diabetes and, much less strongly, to heart disease. Twenty years ago an epidemiologist, Geoffrey Rose, said that it was impossible to determine whether smoking was importantly linked to heart disease because, increasingly, people who smoked were different from those who did not – both in their lifestyles and their origins. He added that, since there were already sound reasons to discourage people from smoking because it damages the lungs, the issue was only significant if a focus on smoking diverted people from following other lines of enquiry in the search for the causes of one of the world's leading causes of death. Which it did.

One evening in the beautiful city of Mysore, India, I stood in a hotel beside a representative of a medical charity. I would like to write that we stared through the open window down on to the maharaja's palaces whose towers gleamed in the moonlight; but the windows had shutters on to keep out the monkeys. I remarked that here in south India heart disease was as common among women as it was among men and women anywhere in the world. My companion, a biologist, replied, 'They must smoke too much.' Since smoking is extremely uncommon among women in south India, I offered a reward of £10 for each woman he saw smoking a cigarette the following day. I did not pay out anything.

The evidence that links the lifestyles of men and women to

their risk of heart disease remains glaringly inconsistent. Disease is common among the vegetarian non-smoking women of south India, and uncommon among the meat-eating, smoking men of southern France. For a non-smoking man with a healthy lifestyle, low blood cholesterol and low blood pressure, the most likely cause of death is still heart disease.

In Britain there were large changes in lifestyle during the Second World War, especially in diet. Food rationing led to major and widespread changes in diet, so that much less fat and sugar were eaten while consumption of fibre rose. Nevertheless, deaths from heart disease among middle-aged men and women continued to rise throughout the war and during the period of post-war rationing. Changes in the lifestyles of adults do not offer satisfactory explanations for the rising epidemics of coronary heart disease that are now occurring in the Third World. Nor do they seem able to explain the decline in the disease that is now occurring in the Western world. In many Western countries the steep rise of heart disease has been followed by a fall; in the USA this has been of the order of one-quarter over twenty years. No parallel changes in lifestyle seem to explain it.

There have been trials in which thousands of people experimentally modified their lifestyles for many months. The benefits have been disappointingly small, with only 8 per cent fewer heart attacks at best. The British Heart Foundation has finally been forced to conclude that 'we shall probably never have proof that a particular lifestyle factor or item of diet is important and those who demand proof before any action are condemning us to wait for ever.'

This is sensible and pragmatic. If there is a possibility that by changing the lifestyles of patients who have had a heart attack their chance of a further attack can be reduced, or their slow descent into a life of heart failure, inability to walk, terrifying breathless nights, swollen ulcerated legs, can be arrested, what doctor will not exhort it? As physicians we are familiar with the need to advise patients in circumstances where there is only limited knowledge. If knowledge subsequently advances, the advice can be changed. Sadly, formulation of policies to prevent heart disease by changing the lifestyles of healthy men and women, and of those already sick – policies based on the best available advice – simultaneously created an orthodoxy. This had little relevance in the wards and clinics of hospitals, other than to imply that a heart attack was partly the patient's fault. I am told that the entrance to an old people's home in California carries the inscription, 'If you die it's your own fault.' Away from hospitals and the care of patients, however, the orthodoxy provided a canopy beneath which sheltered the diverse group of research workers who studied heart disease. Statisticians, biochemists, population scientists and experimentalists stood together to protect the notion that heart disease results from the unhealthy lifestyles of Westernised adults. This view of why one person develops the disease while another does not leaves a great deal to be explained: the explanation offered was genes.

CHALLENGING ORTHODOXY

My colleagues and I in the Medical Research Council Unit at the University of Southampton made a map of England and Wales. We divided the countries into the 1366 areas used for local government. From death certificates we determined the number of deaths from heart disease that had occurred in each area over a period of eleven years from 1968 to 1978. During this time almost 1 million people died from heart disease. To give a death rate, the number of deaths in each area was related to the number of men and women living there. This averaged 627 deaths per 10,000 men each year and 231 deaths per 10,000 women. The rates varied widely across the country. When each area was classified as either high, average or low, and accordingly marked in as red, white or green, the map resembled a political map. The red areas, and most of the white areas, were in the north and west; in the historically poor areas of the country, the towns that became the focus of the Industrial Revolution, and the poor farmlands, the strongholds of the Socialist Party. The green areas with low rates were in the south and east, wealthy county towns and rich farmlands, that traditionally vote Conservative. A line drawn between the mouths of two rivers, the Humber and Severn, neatly defined the boundary between high above and low below.

When our map was published the existence of a north-south divide in heart disease within England and Wales, with consequent differences in life expectancy, was already known, though not described in the detail we had shown. Someone had calculated that if every part of the country had the low rates of heart disease found in the rural areas along the south-eastern seaboard, the nation's life expectancy would increase by several years. Indeed, the saving of years of life would exceed what would be achieved by the immediate and permanent abolition of cancer, for many people die of heart disease in the prime of their lives, while cancer usually kills older people.

Our map demonstrated a profound paradox. Heart disease has increased rapidly as Western populations have become wealthier and better nourished. Why, then, has it settled most heavily among poorer people living in worse conditions? What is happening in the red areas? Why has this same link with poverty emerged elsewhere in Europe and in the USA?

By the time we became engaged with this it was clear that there was no simple answer. Though parodied as the land of fish and chips and beer, people in the north of England – apart from a tendency to eat less fruit and vegetables – eat much the same food as people in the south. Surveys had failed to show a north-south divide in smoking, obesity or exercise habits. All that had been found was that people in the north had higher blood pressures. It remained possible, of course, that there was some unsuspected environmental hazard in the north, or some protective influence in the south, and much attention had been given to the idea that the hard drinking water in the south, full of calcium and magnesium, protected people against heart disease. This was

l.

ere was no single aspect of lifestyle that characterised s northerners were exposed to a cocktail of adversity ments would never be identified. A government committee, set up to examine the inequalities in health across the country, had in effect shrugged its shoulders and concluded that 'much, we feel, can only be understood in terms of the more diffuse consequences of the class structure'. Such writing echoed the 'miasma' theory for malaria. Before its transmission by mosquitoes was discovered, the disease was attributed to the miasma, or bad air, of marshlands. Malaria literally means bad air. When distinguished medical scientists are forced into state-ments about 'diffuse consequences', it may be that an important clue has been overlooked.

Inevitably thoughts turned to genes. These were welcome thoughts in that they brought with them the concept that some people might be more vulnerable than others to whatever was causing heart disease and diabetes. But why should genes causing a disease that was proving fatal to millions of people exist? Harmful genes tend to be eliminated from populations by the processes of 'natural selection' described by Charles Darwin. Why should so many people carry genes that would undermine their health in later life? A favoured speculation was that at some point in our evolutionary history – and the Stone Age was often preferred – the genes were beneficial. Perhaps they had enabled people to withstand famine but became a liability when food became plentiful.

These seemed unattractive ideas, historically and biologically. When Britain staged the first Industrial Revolution it centred on the coal seams in the north and west of the country. Coal was necessary to power the machines. The impoverished people who were drawn into the coal-bearing land came not only from the surrounding countryside but from all over the country, including the southern counties. This argues against people in the north having a unique genetic make-up which has led to their high rates of heart disease. And the argument that people who now live in poor conditions are genetically disadvantaged has a tarnished history, to which later chapters will return. Meanwhile, one can reflect on what possible coincidence of mischance caused the poor of the Western world to have been doubly cursed – by poverty and by defective genes.

And then there is the honey bee. The eggs in a beehive which produce either queens or small worker bees have the same genes. When they hatch, the larvae are fed on jelly secreted by the workers. The larva that will become a queen is fed on royal jelly, containing fat, protein, vitamins and sugar. The larvae that will become workers are fed on diluted 'worker' jelly and they are fed less often. It is the food, not the genes, that determine the destiny of a bee. Royal jelly switches on one group of genes, worker jelly another. Genes do not simply switch themselves on and make proteins like automatons. Most of the genes in our bodies are silent and inactive. Whether genes become active depends on what else is happening within the body. Ideas about genes consigning people to red and white areas on the map of heart disease therefore seemed simplistic.

A final reason for rejecting this is a pragmatic one. Though almost every day we read in the newspapers that someone has discovered the genes for a rare disease, or the gene for happiness, or intelligence, there have been few reports of the genes for heart disease, or for diabetes, other than rare forms of the disorders. It is proving not to be as simple as geneticists once thought it might be.

The simplest interpretation of our map was that two influences are required to produce heart disease: one is associated with prosperity and makes the disease increase as countries Westernise; the other is associated with poverty and created the red areas. The poverty factor does not seem to be related to the way people behave in adult life. Poorer people in poorer places are not more exposed to harmful influences – perhaps they are more vulnerable if they are exposed? Perhaps the Western diet, obesity or some other prosperity factor does more damage to poorer people? If so, what could be the origin of the vulnerability? Why should the poor lack resilience to the challenges of prosperity?

There are better explanations of vulnerability to heart disease than that it is rooted in the existence of as yet unidentified genes, explanations that rest on the biological principles that command human development. This is the story of this book. The general notion that the poor are more vulnerable to disease is familiar:

the Black Death and consumption carried off more paupers than gentry. That people are constitutionally vulnerable to the agents of modern disease is also familiar: I am indifferent to the pollen count on a summer's day, but it may profoundly change the well-being of my neighbour, who gets asthma. What is new is the idea that poverty makes people vulnerable to prosperity, to Westernisation.

The hypothesis that poorer people have more heart disease because they are more vulnerable, rather than because they live in an unhealthy way, is perceived as a challenge to the orthodoxy. To some it is also politically inconvenient because responsibility for their ill health cannot be laid at the patient's door.

VULNERABLE OR RESILIENT?

Some early thoughts on the vulnerability of poorer people to heart disease had come from a Norwegian family doctor, Anders Forsdahl. In the long winter evenings of northern Norway, he pondered why people living above the Arctic Circle had death rates that were 25 per cent higher than those in other parts of Norway. The weather was worse, but social and economic conditions were similar to those elsewhere in the country. He concluded the high death rates must be a legacy of the place's history, of events during the childhood of the adult population. Like most good ideas it had occurred to others before him. Statistical studies of mortality in Britain in the early years of the last century had shown that each succeeding generation had lower death rates at each age than the generation before. It was as though 'each generation is endowed with a vitality peculiarly its own, which persistently manifests itself through the succeeding stages of its existence'.

Forsdahl found that the highest death rates from heart disease in northern Norway were occurring among immigrants from Finland. Their lifestyles were similar to those of their neighbours, but in the past these immigrant communities had had poorly paid occupations, had lived in more crowded homes and had been more vulnerable to the famines that occurred periodically. He concluded that poor living conditions in childhood, followed by prosperity in adult life, predisposed men and women to heart disease.

Forsdahl did not pursue his ideas further. His best-known paper is entitled 'Are poor living conditions in childhood and adolescence an important risk factor for arteriosclerotic heart disease?'. The short answer is that they are not. But he had realised that the occurrence of heart disease is not driven by diet, smoking and other behaviour in adult life, though these may contribute to it. He carried ideas about the origins of heart disease back from the lifestyles of adults to the living conditions of children. A further step back was required, however, from children to babies.

IN THE WOMB

A baby grows through the division of its cells. Starting as one cell, the fertilised egg, as it changes from egg, to embryo, to baby, passes through forty-two cycles of cell division. After birth only a further five cycles of division are needed to change the infant into an adult. This makes an important point. Much of the development of the human body is complete before birth. It is only capable of limited change thereafter. The poet William Blake wrote, 'Man brings all that he has or can have into the world with him. Man is born like a garden ready planted and sown.' Much of what we are, our unique individual selves, is established before we are born. Chapter 3 describes how it is established by the interplay between our genes and the environment that our mothers afford us in the womb. Could the vulnerability of poorer people be established in the womb, by an adverse environment during this most critical stage of the body's development?

One reason why we decided to pursue this was the existence of a glaring inconsistency in our map. London was deep green, having among the lowest rates of heart disease in Britain. Yet historically much of London was poor, the London described by

Dickens. I have before me a photograph of children in the East End in 1912. They are waiting for free food. They are dirty and barefoot. One boy has shoes but his toes are sticking out above the soles. Why did such children have low rates of heart disease in their later lives?

There is no doubt that babies born in less affluent families are vulnerable. They are smaller than those born in more affluent families and more of them die. At the time when the people whose deaths were shown on our maps were born, infants died in large numbers. During the First World War the Bishop of London wrote, 'While nine soldiers died every hour in 1915, twelve babies died every hour, so that it was more dangerous to be a baby than a soldier.' As for everyone else, when infants died a certificate of death was made out, stating the date and cause of death (the word 'infant' is used to distinguish a baby after birth from one in the womb, and the term ceases at one year after birth). Much is known about the deaths of infants in those days, not only the immediate medical causes, but the social conditions which led to them. We wondered if the numbers of infant deaths from place to place across England and Wales could be used as a map of vulnerability, and whether this map might match that of heart disease in the same generation. Could the different experiences of babies explain the north-south divide in heart disease? In the attic of the British Medical Association library I found a map of infant mortality made in 1910. The resemblance to our map of heart disease was astonishing.

With my colleague Clive Osmond, a statistician, I computerised published information about the numbers and causes of infant deaths for the years 1921 to 1925; before that time numbers of deaths, but not their causes, had been reported. We examined each of the official 212 groupings of places that were used – all the large towns within each of the fifty-nine counties grouped together, all the smaller towns, all the rural areas and the London boroughs. When finally we were able to relate the number of deaths per thousand infants to death rates from heart disease the results were clear: across the country, in both men and women, the rates of heart disease in any place were predicted by the proportion of babies who had died before the age of one year. The prediction was equally good in large towns, small towns or the countryside. It was extraordinary. The prediction was, however, less good for London. Solutions to the London riddle came from the next stage of the analysis – examination of the causes of infant death.

In those days infants died because of overcrowding, which led to bronchitis, pneumonia, measles and other airborne infections. They died because of poor sanitation and hygiene, which led to diarrhoea; they died because their mothers were too poor and underfed, and they themselves were born too small and puny to survive for more than a few days when the womb's protection was removed. Since different living conditions caused infants to die from different disorders, we wondered if heart disease was linked to a particular cause of infant death and whether we could use this to move away from 'diffuse effects of the class system' to a more precise understanding of how the social environment altered health. Could we solve the riddle of London, where living conditions for children had been every bit as bad as in the northern towns?

Infants who died because their mothers were undernourished and because they were small usually did so in the first month, the newborn stage. Official figures distinguished these deaths from those occurring later, from one month to one year. They did so because the two differ fundamentally. Newborn babies die because life in the womb has given them insufficient vitality to survive after birth. They die because their mothers were unable to nourish them. Some of the babies of poorly nourished mothers die in the womb and are stillborn, others die soon after birth. In contrast, babies who die after one month die not through adversity in the womb but because of poor conditions in the world into which they are born, poor housing, crowding, poor feeding. Was it, we asked, in poor nutrition in the womb or in poor living conditions after birth that the seeds of heart disease were sown?

The result was clear. Heart disease was more strongly predicted by deaths among newborn babies than by deaths during later infancy. Heart disease originated in the womb, though poor living conditions during infancy also seemed to play a role. The weaker association between deaths during later infancy and heart disease in the same generation was largely due to London which, as expected, had high death rates among its infants beyond one month of age, but exceptionally low death rates among its newborn. Why? Rutherford, the physicist, is said to have advised a young scientist, 'If you have a new idea go into a bar and explain it to the barmaid. If she cannot understand it, neither do you.' Scientific ideas should be capable of clear and simple formulation. I do not know a barmaid willing to listen to ideas about vulnerability to heart disease being acquired in the womb; but my family were willing and it was not difficult to explain these ideas. 'What about London?' was an early question.

LONDON

Writing of the London poor, Charles Booth, who mapped the social conditions of every street in London in 1889, recorded that, 'Their life is the life of savages with vicissitudes of extreme hardship and occasional excess. Their food is of the coarsest description, and their only luxury is drink.' In this harsh world many babies died after one month of age, but amid the savagery pregnant mothers and newborn babies were unusually safe. How could this be? The answer is that many of the mothers were not born in London, but came from the fertile farmland of southern England. As teenage girls they, 'the cream of the youth of the villages', were attracted to London by the high wages paid to domestic servants. Servants in London shared the food of the rich. Elsewhere in the country poor living conditions and high death rates among babies after one month of age coexisted with high death rates among newborn babies, because the poor living conditions impaired the nutrition, physique and health of the girls who grew up in them. Not, however, in London – many of whose girls were immigrants.

The low death rates among their newborn babies are today reflected in low rates of heart disease and are part of a general relation that extends across the whole country. Recognition of the importance of life in the womb does not detract from the role of living conditions in infancy and early childhood. They too play a role. Whereas, however, the suggestion that events in childhood influence the development of heart disease had been made before, our focus on mothers and babies was new.

MOTHERS

Dramatic confirmation of the mother's importance came when we compared the past distribution of deaths among mothers during pregnancy – so-called maternal mortality – across the country with the present distribution of heart disease. In Britain maternal mortality remained at a disturbingly high level from the late nineteenth century until the mid-1930s. 'A deep, dark and continuous stream of mortality', as it was described. The distribution of maternal mortality across the country was similar to that of death rates in newborn babies. If mothers had poor physique and health, and were badly nourished, they as well as their babies were more likely to die during pregnancy from conditions such as toxaemia, during labour from haemorrhage and difficulties in giving birth as a consequence of pelvises misshapen by childhood rickets. From place to place, across the country, the numbers of maternal deaths in the past predicted death rates from heart disease in the generation born around that time.

The only other disease for which the map was similar to that of heart disease was stroke. The word 'stroke' is used for damage to the brain resulting from lack of blood flow – due to the pipes, the arteries, bursting or becoming blocked by blood clots. Both heart disease and stroke are linked to hardening of the arteries, in either the heart or the brain. High blood pressure predisposes to both of them and blood pressure levels in the north had been shown to be higher than those in the south. Whereas, however, heart disease is a Western disease, rising with affluence, stroke is a Third World disease, commonest in China and Japan, declining as living conditions improve. Rates of stroke were even more closely predicted by past maternal mortality than was heart disease. Unlike heart disease, however, the living conditions into which a baby was born, as indicated by deaths in babies from one month to one year, seemed to have little effect on stroke.

Analyses of maternal deaths carried out in the 1920s had shown that places with high maternal death rates during pregnancy or delivery were characterised by women having poor physique – they were thin and stunted. It was not only what they ate or did not eat during pregnancy, but what they brought to pregnancy as a result of poor childhood nutrition, rickets during infancy and employment in manual work, in industry or in the fields, from an early age. It seemed that a baby who in later life developed stroke might have responded not only to the mother's surroundings and diet during the pregnancy, but also to her lifetime's experience.

These observations in Britain may throw light on a riddle that has puzzled scientists in the USA for decades. For a long time strokes have been more common in the south-east of the USA than anywhere else in the country. The so-called 'stroke belt' comprises a contiguous cluster of states in the south-east, with Indiana jutting upwards from it. The high death rates from stroke affect men and women, blacks and whites, with especially high rates in young black people. They are not explained by differences in the quality of medical care. The prevalence of hypertension, the main biological risk factor for stroke, has also been shown to be higher in the south-east. Despite intensive investigation there is no agreed explanation for the existence of the stroke belt. There seems to be no common lifestyle differences that would explain it, nor are there differences in dietary intakes of salt, potassium or other nutrients thought to be linked to raised blood pressure.

There are, however, two important clues. The first is that within the stroke belt stroke mortality is highest in people with poor education, low incomes and unskilled occupations. Indeed, there is no excess of stroke mortality in the south-east among affluent people. So the pattern of disease is not so much a 'belt' of increased stroke across the whole region but a 'necklace' of different levels of risk.

The second clue is that within the south-east the highest rates of stroke occur among people who were born there. South Carolina has had the highest stroke mortality in the United States for many years, with rates 50 to 60 per cent above the national average. Stroke is most common among people who were born in South Carolina, especially black people. It is somewhat less common in those born elsewhere in the south-east, and least common in those born outside the south-east. These findings are supported by an analysis of deaths in New York City, where stroke is unusually common among black people. This is, however, largely confined to black people who were born in the southern states but migrated to the north-east. These two clues suggest that the origins of the stroke belt may lie in events in early life that are linked to poverty.

In the stroke belt malnutrition was common around the turn of the last century as a result of the social changes which began in the Civil War and continued until the depression. Vitamin deficiency and the diseases it causes were widespread. Pellagra, for example, in which people become demented, and have chronic diarrhoea and skin troubles, was still common among poor people in the south until the 1930s. Their diets of pork fat and 'hominy grits' made from corn were deficient in one of the B vitamins, nicotinic acid. A high rate of low birthweight persists in the south to this day and, as would be expected, this is linked to a high death rate among newborn babies. The stroke belt may therefore be the legacy of events portrayed in *Gone with the Wind*.

STURDIER AND HEALTHIER MOTHERS

An impressive feature of these geographic analyses was the ability of past infant death rates to predict differences in the rates of heart disease even within one county, or between neighbouring towns. One day, I sat in my office and toured the map of Lincolnshire, a rural county in the east of England. As I proceeded from one small town to the next the correspondence between the rates of heart disease and the past death rates in newborn babies seemed remarkable. It deepened our conviction that in the close geographical association between the deaths of babies and death from heart disease in the same generation we were seeing a strong biological effect. My wife and I took a holiday in Lancashire, an industrial county in the north, devoid of green low heart disease areas. We visited Burnley, where John Clegg lived, and had an insight into the social conditions that jeopardised the nutrition and health of young women, and diminished the vitality of generations of babies. We began to progress beyond 'the diffuse consequences of the class structure'.

BACK TO BURNLEY

Burnley is one of three Lancashire towns – Burnley, Nelson and Colne – situated side by side on the western slopes of the Pennine Hills. The towns developed in the nineteenth century as centres for cotton weaving. Burnley is in the valley, where two rivers meet. Nelson and Colne lie above it. For the six miles from the centre of Burnley through Nelson and up to Colne there is hardly a break in the line of houses, yet our map showed that there were large differences in the rates of heart disease in the towns. In Burnley rates of heart disease and stroke were 20 per cent above the national average, making it one of the most unhealthy towns in the country. Rates in Nelson, however, were around the average, while in Colne they were intermediate between the other two towns. In contrast, deaths from lung cancer, indicating the frequency of cigarette smoking, were at average or below average levels in each of the towns.

All three towns are among the poorer towns of England and Wales. At the time we studied them, living conditions in the towns were similar. Many people were employed as manual workers – Nelson, the healthiest town, having the highest proportion. In all three towns the level of crowding in the homes was above the national average: around half the families lived in houses with fewer than five rooms, compared with a national average of one-third. Incomes were low and the number of families owning a car was fewer than average. The towns shared the same medical services, the hospital being in Burnley, where John Clegg went.

Historically, however, the towns were very different. Through the first half of the last century babies in Burnley had among the highest death rates of babies anywhere in the country. During the First World War one in every six babies born in Burnley died in infancy. A few miles up the hill, in Nelson, only one in twelve babies died. In Colne it was one in eight. The excess deaths in Burnley and Colne occurred both in the newborn period and during later infancy. They reflected the poor physique and health of women, and the poor living conditions into which babies were born.

In all three towns at that time employment levels were high and wages good, and remained so for many years. The poverty was not lack of money, but of another kind. Almost half of all the women and girls in the three towns worked in the weaving mills. In Burnley and Colne many of the women were from the second or third generation of Lancashire industrial workers, and had grown up in crowded streets in small unsanitary houses. The houses were damp, especially those in Burnley built in the early 1800s in the marshy valley, made damper yet by water leaking down from the canal embankment above them. Some houses were built 'back to back' with no means of ventilation to the outside air. They lacked any facilities for the storage of food and milk. In 1912, one in every four babies born into these back-to-back houses died before reaching one year of age, mostly as a result of diarrhoea. Predictably, there were those who said that these terrible death rates reflected the fecklessness of the people who lived in the houses. Yet when families from back-to-back houses were resettled into 'through' houses, adequately ventilated, far fewer babies died.

The young women who grew up in these conditions, and went to work in the mills at the age of ten, were stunted. When their babies were born they were small and many died. Many of these mothers had to return to full-time work just a few days after having had a baby. A report on another Lancashire town,

Preston, described a day in the life of a young mother working in the mills. 'She would have to get up at 5.30 a.m., wrap the baby in a shawl and take it to a nurse who would care for it during the day. These baby minders had little concern for the children in their care and often drugged them heavily. At 8.30 the mother would rush back from the mill to breastfeed her baby and would probably snatch a piece of bread for herself on the way back. At midday she would rush back to feed the baby and then work on until 5.30 p.m. This went on day after day until mother and baby were completely debilitated.' There were no crèches in the mills of Burnley and Colne. Usually the mother's return to work was soon followed by complete weaning and the infant, together with other children in the family below school age, was placed in the care of an untrained 'minder' who was paid by the mother. 'In view of the fact that so many mothers are anxious, for the sake of the wages, to get back to employment in the mills as soon as possible after childbirth, a large proportion of children born in Burnley are deprived of the advantages of breastfeeding after the first few weeks of life.'

Nelson developed more recently than Burnley and Colne, and its population increased eightfold between 1871 and 1911. Most of its people were immigrants from nearby rural areas, especially from rural Yorkshire on the other side of the Pennine Hills. 'This fact,' wrote a report in 1914, 'has an important bearing on the question of infantile mortality, owing to the general good health and the habits of cleanliness and thrift characteristic of these immigrants from rural districts.' The women were described as 'sturdier and healthier' than those in Burnley and Colne.

The houses in Nelson were better than those in the other two towns, newer and more spacious. Sanitary conditions were also better than those in the other towns. In Nelson the women kept the streets outside their houses clean: 'more water being said to be used for this purpose in Nelson than in any other town in Lancashire'. Mothers continued to breastfeed their infants for longer than in the other towns.

BACK TO JOHN CLEGG

Though his liking for fried lunches and his sedentary job may have contributed to John Clegg's heart attack, it seemed that the complete explanation had to go back to his development in the womb when the systems of his body were established, back to his mother who nourished him in the womb and her own childhood, back, perhaps, to his mother's mother who nourished her, back to the social conditions produced down the generations by the Industrial Revolution and further back yet to the genes he acquired from the long march of man's evolutionary progression from fish to frogs to four-legged animals to humans, genes which may become activated or not, depending on conditions during development.

FURTHER RESEARCH

The maps had brought us to a new point of departure for research. It seemed that heart disease and stroke originated through a vulnerability acquired in the womb and during infancy. The diseases were more common in places where, historically, babies were small at birth and died in large numbers because their mothers were poorly nourished. Both diseases were linked to hardening of the arteries and raised blood pressure, which might originate in the womb. Heart disease was a Western disease increasing with affluence. Vulnerability acquired through adversity in the womb could not be the sole cause. A second influence, linked to prosperity and presumably acting after birth, also had to be necessary.

We looked at the pattern of the heart disease epidemics in the West – a steep rise over several decades followed by a fall. Was the rise due to the prosperity factor combined with the poverty factor acting in the womb, and the fall due to the progressive disappearance of the poverty factor or factors, the disappearance of thin, stunted, poorly nourished mothers and their undernourished babies? Was the prosperity factory evenly distributed across the country, experienced by everyone as the Industrial Revolution improved the lot of all; while adversity in the womb shaped the north-south divide and left a legacy that may endure for several generations, even though the weaving mills of Burnley closed many years ago? An inheritance paid for in the intensive care units of our hospitals, in premature disability, in the deaths of many people?

The evidence supporting this hypothesis was circumstantial, the geographical coincidence of death rates at two different stages of life – infancy and old age. To advance these ideas it was necessary to follow the course of individuals' lives, to see whether the lives of people who had low birthweight and poor living conditions during infancy were ended prematurely by heart disease.

2

The Internal Environment

MEDICAL ARCHAEOLOGY

Birthweight is a useful marker of conditions in the womb. If conditions are unfavourable because the mother is badly nourished, or ill, or for other reasons unable to transfer food to her baby, the baby will grow more slowly and have a lower birthweight than a baby in favourable conditions. If heart attacks are more common among people living in poorer places because adverse conditions in the womb made them more vulnerable to the disease, one would predict that the disease would be more common among people who had had a low birthweight. Similarly, growth during infancy is a useful marker of conditions after birth, and if adverse conditions during infancy make people more vulnerable to the disease it will be more common among people who had poor growth between birth and one year.

To test this idea has required studies of a kind never undertaken before. It has been necessary to find large groups of men and women aged fifty years or more, the age above which heart attacks are common, whose weight was recorded at birth and for whom there would be information about living conditions in infancy.

During the 1980s my colleagues at the University of Southampton searched archives and hospital record departments throughout Britain, looking for maternity and infant welfare records from the early years of the century. Many were found. Some were in large collections preserved over many years; in others there were no more than a few hundred records kept by one clinic or even one midwife. Some were detailed and some perfunctory. Some were in archives; others were in lofts, sheds, garages, boiler rooms, or flooded basements. The largest set of records was made by health visitors in the county of Hertfordshire.

THE HERTFORDSHIRE RECORDS

In the early years of the twentieth century, there was widespread concern about the physical deterioration of the British people. One in ten infants died before they were a year old and many of those who survived reached adult life in poor health. During 1902, reports in the national press claimed that up to two-thirds of the young men who volunteered to fight in the Boer War in South Africa (1899 to 1902) had been rejected because of unsatisfactory physique. An Interdepartmental Committee set up in 1903 drew a shocking picture of the nation's children – malnourished, poorly housed, deprived. Moreover, the birth rate was declining. The Medical Officer of Health for Hertfordshire, a county just to the north of London, writing at around this time, stated,

> Hertfordshire does less than forty out of the fifty-five counties to perpetuate the national stock; for England and Wales the birth-rate has for thirty-three years been steadily declining, only two Continental countries (Belgium and France) having lower birth-rates, while that for Japan is increasing and is now ahead of every white race but Russia and three of the Balkan States. The new census figures show a lower rate of increase than in any decennium of the last century. This decay must betoken the doom of modern civilisation as it did that of Rome and Greece, unless some new moral or physical factors arise to defeat it. [He added] it is of national importance that the life of every infant be vigorously conserved.

Responding to this challenge a young woman, Ethel Margaret Burnside, the county's first ever 'Chief Health Visitor and Lady Inspector of Midwives' set up an 'army' of trained nurses to attend women in childbirth and to advise mothers on how to keep their infants healthy after birth. From 1911 onwards, when women in Hertfordshire had their babies, they were attended by a midwife. She recorded the birthweight. The local health visitor was informed. She went to the baby's home at intervals through-out infancy in order to advise the mother, and recorded the baby's illnesses and development on a card. When the infant was one year old she weighed it again and the card was handed in to the county offices, where the details were carefully transferred into ledgers. The ledgers were maintained until 1945, many years after Miss Burnside had retired. The health visitors continued to visit the children's homes periodically until they went to school and details of the children's illnesses are also in the ledgers.

Surprisingly little is known about this remarkable woman whose foresight and dedication gave us the Hertfordshire records. The only known photograph of her was taken when she was seventeen years old. She was born in 1877, one of six children. Her father was rector of the village of Hertingfordbury. After training as a nurse at St George's Hospital, London, she became Lady Inspector of Midwives for Hertfordshire in 1905. We know that she worked energetically. 'The cyclometer of my bicycle registered 2,921 miles for the year,' she reported. In 1910 she was made a Queen's Nurse and the county nursing association recorded its 'high appreciation' of her 'unremitting labours'. In 1913 she persuaded the County Council to buy her a car. It was 9.5 horsepower and she called it 'little hero'. She is remembered as a reserved but formidable woman. The Clerk to the County Council was in fear of her and would make himself immediately available if he knew she was in the building and wished to see him.

We became aware of the Hertfordshire ledgers in 1986. Hitherto we had only found maternity records, which gave birth-weights but no information about growth during infancy. Here in Hertfordshire, beyond anything we could have expected, were birthweights and weights at one year systematically recorded for thousands of people. We discovered that those covering six villages in the eastern part of the county had been lodged in the

County Record Office. I hastened there. At first the office was unwilling to release them, even for the purposes of medical research. The midwives and health visitors had at times written harsh comments about the mothers' habits and skill – 'mother feckless', 'dirty home': it was better that such comments were not made public as some of the mothers must still be alive.

By a remarkable coincidence I had lived in one of the six villages during the war, a London boy sent to the countryside with his mother and brother to escape German bombs, part of one of the largest movements of children in history. From time to time my father returned from war service to visit us and my sister was born in 1943 – an event recorded in the Burnside ledgers. When the Record Office learnt that the research team was to be led by a local man, access to the ledgers was granted. Though the logic of this decision was unclear, we returned to Southampton with the ledgers and deposited them in the only safe archive the university possessed – the archive that holds the private papers of the Duke of Wellington. While the Duke's papers must be important, Britain's Chief Medical Officer of Health at the time likened the Hertfordshire records to the Tomb of Tutankhamun. In my sister's case the tomb was empty. My mother was notably independent and did not allow her baby to be weighed. Neither did my god-mother who, with her children, also refugees from London, shared our house and had a baby at around this time. Happily very few women took my mother's hostile view of Margaret Burnside's nurses and the records were remarkably complete.

In the first study 15,000 men and women born in the county before 1930 were traced: 3000 of them were already dead, almost half of them from heart disease or the disorders related to it. We found that, as our maps had predicted, a disproportionate num-ber of these deaths had occurred among people who had had low birthweights. The risk of a fatal heart attack in later life halved between people who weighed 5 pounds (2.3 kg) or less at birth and those who weighed 10 pounds (4.6 kg) or more. It was not that the smallest babies had high death rates and everyone else was similar. Rather, there was a progressive fall across the range of birthweights so that 7-pound babies were at lower risk than

6-pound babies, 8-pound babies at lower risk than 7. Later studies have confirmed this and also shown that it is not babies who were small because they were born prematurely who are at increased risk of later heart disease, but babies who had grown slowly. Today, 40,000 babies born in Hertfordshire before the Second World War have been traced and are part of a continuing medical research project.

We also looked at whether the people's growth during infancy, the first year after birth, had influenced their risk of heart disease. Again, as our maps had predicted, men who only put on weight slowly during infancy had had more heart disease. The risk of the disease among men who weighed only 18 pounds (8.2 kg) or less was three times that among men who weighed 27 pounds (12.3 kg) or more. Even among the men whose birth-weights were above the average of 7.9 pounds (3.6 kg), poor weight gain during infancy increased, doubled, the risk of heart disease. Among girls, poor weight gain during infancy did not increase the risk of heart disease. The growth of girls is less vulnerable to adversity than the growth of boys. They maintain their rate of growth more doggedly than boys. Recently we have begun to learn that girls who later develop heart disease sustain their growth during infancy but, in persisting poor living conditions, their growth falters after the age of one year. This insight is still at an early stage.

Meanwhile, among boys, were we seeing two different pathways to heart disease, the London path and the Burnley path? The London path, the green path, the low road began after birth. Buxom country girls, who had come to the city to work as domestic servants, had large babies of above average weight. Once born, however, their mothers having left the comforts of the homes of the rich, the 'savagery' of the world into which they were thrust bore in on them. Poor housing, overcrowding and poor sanitation led to recurrent illness, and the infants did not thrive, especially in the difficult period around weaning. The Burnley path to heart disease, the red path, the high road, began before birth. Stunted mothers, badly nourished since childhood, working in the mills since the age of ten, had small, thin, unhealthy babies. Born into small, unhygienic, overcrowded houses, these little babies struggled through infancy; many died. Those who survived were at high risk of heart disease. The combination of poor conditions in the womb and poor conditions after birth was more lethal than poor conditions only after birth.

Though this integration of the Hertfordshire findings with the maps may turn out to be too simple – and it probably will – we began to think about the different pathways to disease. The same disease might originate through different paths and, though the ultimate, fatal event – blockage of the arteries supplying the heart muscle – might be the same, the biological processes leading to the event might differ: processes, for example, linked to high blood pressure, or to raised blood cholesterol, or to both. This book will return repeatedly to the theme of pathways.

ORTHODOXY STRIKES BACK

We were amazed by these early results. The weights of babies and infants recorded long ago in cottages and terraced houses, measured by the light of candles and lanterns, using the simplest of weighing scales, were predicting heart disease fifty years later. To predict threefold differences in risk of heart disease is a challenge when people are already middle-aged and attending a surgery or clinic. Unsurprisingly, perhaps, when these findings were published in medical journals, they were not greeted with universal enthusiasm. By this time, in the late 1980s, the orthodoxy that heart disease resulted from the unhealthy lifestyles of Westernised men and women had taken root deeply. There were letters of complaint and people walked out of meetings when we presented our findings. One Saturday morning the BBC news announced that our findings had been disproved – though by what was not clear. I was challenged to public debates.

When I was a young doctor I worked in Uganda and I often had to visit Jinja, the source of the River Nile, which pours in a cataract from Lake Victoria. A plaque commemorates its discovery by John Hanning Speke, who overcame all manner of difficulties before finally returning home. Richard Burton did not believe that he had discovered the source of the Nile and challenged him to a public debate. It never happened because Speke shot himself the day before. Burton, being the better debater, would presumably have won, but to what purpose? The source of the Nile is where it is and will not be changed by a show of hands in London. In science, uncertainties need to be resolved by more research, not oratory.

So we declined debate and continued the work. The development of any new field of research is greatly helped by the interest and support of a major journal. The *British Medical Journal* published many of the earlier papers and later collected them together as a book. The University of Southampton championed the research. Government funds and medical charities, including the British Heart Foundation and the Dunhill Medical Trust, funded it.

An interesting response to the Hertfordshire findings was the suggestion that little babies were born into different kinds of homes from big babies, poorer homes, perhaps, with worse educated parents. As a result they grew up to have worse, less 'healthy' lifestyles, and it was these lifestyles, the argument ran, that led to their high rates of heart disease rather than their small size at birth. However, there was little in Hertfordshire to support this idea. Whereas the size of the house into which the babies were born, the number of other people living there, their fathers' income, the families' living standards all had an effect on their growth during infancy, it did not affect their growth in the womb. This, as will be described in later chapters, depends on the mother and her origins. Later studies by other groups addressed the issue carefully. A detailed study of 15,000 men and women born in Uppsala, Sweden, and a large study of 100,000 nurses in the USA showed that people who had had a low birthweight were at greater risk of developing heart disease, irrespective of their subsequent lifestyles or living conditions. This is not to say that living conditions after birth do not have an effect. They do but only, it seems, on some people, on people following particular pathways to disease. We will return to this.

THE INTERNAL ENVIRONMENT

That small babies, even those born after a normal-length pregnancy, are vulnerable is not in question. More of them die. Babies of 4 pounds (1.8 kg) are ten times more likely to die after birth than 9-pound (4.1 kg) babies. They die because their unsuccessful struggle to grow in a poor environment renders them unable to adjust to the new and dangerous world outside the womb. Within minutes of birth the baby casts off its single lifeline, the placenta, and must rapidly establish others; breast milk must be absorbed through the untested digestive system; air absorbed through the lungs; the kidneys must begin to clear the body's waste. Bigger babies are more fit, better able to achieve the internal upheavals by which their lives are preserved.

But why should small babies be at greater risk of heart disease in later life, long after the transition from the womb to the outside world has been accomplished? One obvious possible explanation arises from the extent to which the body is complete at birth. We bring into the world, for example, all the kidney cells we will ever have, all the muscle cells. Thereafter we can only enlarge what we have. Small babies have fewer cells than large babies, less functional capacity. As we age we lose cells. In people who were small at birth functional capacity may become critical: the kidneys may no longer be able to maintain blood pressure at normal levels, the muscles may be too weak to sustain activity.

It must, however, be more complex than that. The organs of the body do not act alone, any more than do the machines in a factory. They act in concert, creating systems such as that which regulates the pressure in the blood system. The flow of blood depends on the coordinated activity of the heart, kidneys, nervous system. Coordination requires signalling by hormones and nerves. Activity requires fuel, provided by the chain of biochemical commands through which the body metabolises food.

Coordinated by the brain, the body's systems maintain an inner constancy in an ever changing world outside. One aspect of maintaining constancy is establishing the amount of hormones that are needed in the blood before particular 'target' tissues respond to their commands. This is achieved by setting the levels of 'receptors' in the cells. The sergeant must shout his commands because some of his troop do not respond to normal speech. During development the receptors in the cells establish a level of sensitivity above which the cell will respond to a hormone. This level is known as the set point. Different tissues have different set points. If the amount of hormone released is small, only tissues with low set points respond. If more hormone is released, other tissues respond as well. This creates a flexible system, one in which the responses to hormonal commands vary – more like the responses of a school outing to the teacher than those of a platoon to the drill sergeant.

Each of us has a unique 'internal environment', or *milieu intérieur* as it was first described by the French physiologist, Claude Bernard. '*La fixité du milieu intérieur*', he wrote, '*est la condition essentielle de la vie libre*': our internal environments condition our response to the external environment. When the fire alarm rings, people respond in all manner of ways. How one person's body responds differs from the responses of another and determines what they feel and what they do. So, more mundanely, do the body's responses to food: some people dispose of surplus food, others store it. We acquire our internal environment during development; thereafter it is relatively constant. For example, the pattern by which a woman produces sex hormones, the amounts, the timing of the pulses by which they are released through the day and night, is unique to her and was established before she was born.

We now know beyond challenge that the internal environments of people who were small at birth differ from those of people who were large. The issue in relation to heart disease is whether these differences involve systems that are known to have a role in the disease.

TRACKING

It is well known that people who develop heart disease tend to have high blood pressure, too much cholesterol in their blood and are less able to store sugar in their muscles, a deficiency that ultimately leads to diabetes. These and other abnormalities, including an increased likelihood of blood clots forming in arteries, are markers that the body is prone to heart disease. However, the link is not necessarily a simple one. The danger of rising blood pressure is not merely that it may rupture the pipes, the arteries, though it may. Heart disease is essentially about the narrowing and clotting up of arteries. As has been described, blood pressure is controlled by a system and it may not be only the pressure, but the malfunction of other parts of the system, that leads to heart disease.

An important question is the extent to which blood pressure, and the levels of cholesterol and sugar in the blood, reflect the lifestyles of men and women, and to what extent they reflect the inner environment. An early intimation that a person's blood pressure level or blood cholesterol might be more than markers of how much salt or fat they consume came from studies of children. Blood pressure and cholesterol levels vary between one child and another, as they do between adults. If levels are measured a number of times as children grow up, those who had the highest levels early on still tend to have the highest levels ten years later. Blood pressure levels track from early childhood to middle age and beyond, and do not simply reflect the stresses and vagaries of our daily lives, though these do have an effect. From the age of six months children maintain their blood cholesterol levels in relation to other children. Put another way, blood pressure levels and cholesterol 'track' from childhood into adult life. This is evidence that they reflect our inner environment, the balance of our body's different functions, the 'homeostasis' that maintains an internal constancy. Less is known about the tracking of blood sugar, because the tests required are more complex, but tracking undoubtedly occurs.

A NEW ARMY OF NURSES

Given that blood pressure, cholesterol and sugar levels reflect our internal environment, as well as the environment in which we live, we needed to know how they related to growth in the womb. Do small babies have higher levels which persist through life and thereby increase their risk of heart disease? To answer this, hundreds of men and women who were born in Hertfordshire and still lived there were invited to attend clinics, which were established in hospitals and doctors' surgeries around the county. Many agreed to do so and have over the years given generously of their time, allowing all manner of intrusions into their privacy. A new army of nurses took the place of Margaret Burnside's. Men and women who had not seen each other since schooldays were reunited in the clinics, as they awaited tests. Their heights, weights and blood pressures were measured, blood tests were carried out to measure cholesterol, blood clotting, how their bodies responded to a sugary drink. The results were dramatic. People who had been small at birth had higher blood pressures and were more likely to have the common form of diabetes which begins in adult life, so-called type 2 diabetes, which for simplicity will be referred to as diabetes. This disorder, but not raised blood pressure, was also linked to poor weight gain in infancy, the 'London path' to heart disease. Small babies had raised blood cholesterol levels, though these were also influenced by growth during infancy, and by whether or not the baby had been breast-fed and for how long.

These findings showed that, irrespective of their current body size, people who were small at birth or during infancy remained biologically different throughout their lives. Again, it was not merely people who were very small babies, weighing less than 5½ pounds (2.5 kg) – a definition of low birthweight commonly used in hospitals – who were different from everyone else. Rather, the 7-pound baby was different from the 8-pound, and the 8-pound different from the 9. Generally, it seemed, the bigger the baby the better its internal environment and its prospects in later life – though there is an important caveat to this because some babies are large because they are fat rather than because they have large heads and long and muscular bodies, and these fat babies are at increased risk of later diabetes.

We found more records in two northern towns: Preston, a former cotton town, and Sheffield, a manufacturing town. We established clinics there. In each town we had collections of detailed maternity records going back fifty years and more. Each newborn baby had been measured in remarkable detail. Not only was it weighed but its length was recorded. Callipers were used to take seven different measures of the baby's head and the placenta was weighed. In Sheffield the circumference of the baby's chest and abdomen were also measured. Using all these measurements we can today produce detailed drawings of these newborn babies that their mothers would have recognised.

We do not know why, all those years ago, in busy delivery rooms where childbirth was frequently attended by disaster, where a baby's progress down the birth canal was often arrested by a misshapen pelvis, a legacy of the mother's childhood rickets, where having given birth, mothers often bled to death, where so many perished that old women in Preston recalled that being admitted to the hospital it seemed as though you had entered pur-gatory, that time was set aside to greet every baby born with a time-consuming ritual of elaborate measurement and recording. Anecdote says that the hospital matron who began all this activity in Preston was jilted. She retreated into the hospital and insisted on attending every delivery, day or night. Her presence commanded the careful record keeping that today allows us to relate people's health to their appearance at birth, to whether they were thin babies or stunted ones, to whether they had large or small heads, to whether they were attached to their mothers by large placentas or small ones. And, in Sheffield, to whether they had a large abdomen or a small one, for much of the abdomen of a newborn baby is taken up by the liver; and the liver regulates how much cholesterol there is in the blood, and babies with large abdomens had lower blood cholesterol levels fifty years later, to which we will return.

The findings in the northern towns confirmed those in

Hertfordshire though, as would be expected, there were interesting differences. The effect of birthweight on blood pressure levels, for example, differed from place to place. But these historically were different places and in biology variation is to be expected. We moved on to attempts to understand in more depth the workings of the internal environment of people who were small at birth.

SWEATING

Why should people who were small at birth be persistently different through their lives? Why do they not recuperate after birth? The sweat glands offer a clue. In the last century Japanese military expansion took their soldiers and settlers into unfamiliar climates. They found that there were wide differences in people's abilities to adapt to hot climates. Physiologists were ordered to study this and found that it was related to the number of functioning sweat glands. Each of us has a different number of functioning sweat glands on our skin. Some of us have many glands, sweat freely and adapt well to hot weather, others less so. It is genetic, would be the fashionable response today, but the Japanese looked more deeply and made an interesting discovery.

At birth the sweat glands are inactive. In the next three years a proportion of them begin to function. In hot countries many become functional, in cold countries only a few. After three years the number that are active is fixed. Glands that are inactive remain so for ever. The story of the sweat gland, first described by the Japanese scientists, illustrates a simple but important phenomenon. Some of the body's systems need to acquire experience from the external environment before they function and assume their final form. The brain is moulded by experience, the development of the sweat glands is triggered by heat. It is neither good nor bad to have few working sweat glands. It is merely appropriate to life in colder places. But if, in later life, the environment changes, it may be a disadvantage. Japanese soldiers who grew up in colder parts of the country struggled when they were sent to the Tropics. For the sweat gland it is the environment after birth that determines its destiny. However, for much of the body, it is the environment before birth, in the womb.

PLASTICITY

The sweat glands research introduces the concept of plasticity during development. The organs and systems of the body are not destined to behave in ways determined at the moment of conception, by the genes. In principle, this has been known for a long while. There are not enough genes to programme the assembly of the world's most complex machine, the human brain. There are numerous experiments in which the physiology and structure of young animals have been permanently and profoundly changed by the simplest of procedures, such as reducing the amount of food given to the mother. Plasticity is a universal quality of living things as they develop and it alters their lifespan and life history.

The common lizard is a successful creature. It inhabits a broad swath of the earth from Spain in the west to the Pacific coast of Russia, from Romania to Scandinavia. Its success is due to its plasticity. In different places it grows and matures at different rates. In France the lizards living at high altitude in the heaths and peat bogs of the Massif Centrale grow more slowly than those living at low altitude in the meadows of Brittany, where it is warmer and food is plentiful. They do not become sexually mature until they are two years old, while those in Brittany become mature at one. They live for three years, while the Brittany lizards die at two. If, after hatching, young lizards from both places are reared in a laboratory in Paris, their lives are identical.

THE FOETAL ORIGINS HYPOTHESIS

Sweat glands and the lizard show that systems of the body are plastic during development, moulded by the environment, and so is the body as a whole: its rate of growth, the age at which it matures, the number of its days. From tracing people in Hertfordshire from birth to death, we know that people who had low birthweight are at increased risk of heart disease. Another pathway to heart disease begins with poor growth during infancy, the result of poor living conditions that lead to recurrent illness and malnutrition. The maps of England and Wales suggested that the principal cause underlying the link between low birthweight and later heart disease was poor maternal nutrition and health, itself the result of the poverty factor, the poor living conditions to which girls and young women were subject. It was now time to put together a formal hypothesis. The 'foetal origins hypothesis' stated that heart disease, stroke, diabetes and hypertension originate through developmental plasticity, in response to undernutrition during foetal life and infancy.

3

The Plastic Baby

DEVELOPMENTAL PLASTICITY

Plasticity is a universal quality of living things as they develop. Within the limits imposed by its genes and by mechanical constraints, each individual has a range of options for its life history and final body form and function. Children today are taller and reach puberty earlier than their parents did – clearly not the result of genetic change but a response to a better environment. Just as each individual alters its behaviour in response to different situations, so does it 'choose' a particular path of growth and development in response to signals or 'cues' from the environment. The genes acquired at conception are capable of producing a range of body sizes, shapes, states and behaviours. These are referred to as 'phenotypes', which describe all aspects of a living thing other than its genetic constitution, or 'genotype'. The formal definition of developmental plasticity is 'the ability of a single genotype to produce more than one alternative form of structure, physiological state or behaviour in response to environmental conditions'. Which phenotype is produced or 'expressed' by a particular genotype depends on the environment at the time. When a man is fleeing from a charging bull, neither the bull nor anyone else is interested in his genotype. The issue is how fast and how far can he run – his phenotype – which is influenced by the food he had and the exercise he took during development.

Plasticity during development may seem at variance with the understanding of genetic inheritance which we have derived from breeding experiments in plants and animals. Until recently genetic considerations have dominated discussions of evolution. Darwin first described how evolution occurs over many generations through natural selection of genes that optimise the fitness of a species in a particular environment, but he was also aware that the environment produces variation within one generation. 'When a variation is of the slightest use to a being,' he wrote, 'we cannot tell how much of it to attribute to the accumulative action of natural selection, and how much to the conditions of life. Thus, it is well known to furriers that animals of the same species have thicker and better fur the more severe the climate is under which they have lived; but who can tell how much of this differ-ence may be due to the warmest-clad individuals having been favoured and preserved during many generations, and how much to the direct action of the severe climate?' Among domestic animals, he noted, cold weather had a direct effect in promoting the growth of hair. Is that why in Mediterranean countries cats look so scraggy?

Natural selection chooses animals that can avoid predators and survive, and are attractive to the opposite sex. 'Fitness' in an animal is measured by reproductive success, by the number of its offspring that live to breed in their turn. The environment is not simply the arena in which natural selection occurs through varying degrees of survival and reproductive success. Rather, it determines which phenotypes are produced and exposed to selection. Developmental plasticity enables the production of phenotypes that are better suited to their environment than would be possible if the same phenotype were produced regard-less of the environment. If, however, the environment during development is replaced by a different environment, as when Japanese soldiers from cold parts of the country went to the Tropics, mismatches may occur.

THE UNDERNOURISHED BABY

Soon after it is fertilised, the egg begins to divide, initially pro-ducing exact replicas of itself, but thereafter producing distinct groups of different cells with different destinies. Development depends on changes in the form and function of cells, so-called differentiation, which enables cells to carry out specialised tasks.

Eight weeks of embryonic development lead to a recognisable human being, though with a large head and only a small body. Most of the tissues and organs have differentiated. The embryo becomes a foetus and the period of fastest growth in a lifetime begins. Growth requires an increase in cell numbers and expansion of existing cells. Different organs have different strategies: the liver enlarges by repeated division of mature cells. Muscle and nerve cells, once formed, are incapable of further division: they last for a lifetime, and can only be enlarged. Visits to the health club do not make new muscle; they expand what is already there. In the last third of pregnancy systems that are essential for independent life after birth – the lungs, kidneys, digestive system – mature. At birth much of the body is completed, primed to take on an altered role after birth and destined to change little, other than by expansion of the cells.

SENSITIVE PERIODS

At the moment of conception every human being has many possible paths of growth before it. What path it follows, what size it attains at birth, depend on the environment, especially the supply of nutrients from the mother. It is unsurprising that this environment will also determine lifelong differences in characteristics such as blood pressure. Numerous observations on animals have shown that undernutrition, hormones and other influences that affect development during what are called 'sensitive' or 'critical' periods in early life permanently alter the structure and function of the body's tissues and systems. The sensitive period in the development of an organ such as the kidney often coincides with the period when its cells are dividing most. Because the timing of this period of rapid division differs from one organ to another, the effects of undernutrition and other adverse influences will depend on their timing.

A striking illustration of sensitive periods is provided by early experiments on rats. When a female rat was given an injection of the male hormone, testosterone, on the fifth day after birth her sexual characteristics developed normally, but she never mated. One injection had irreversibly altered the pattern of release of the hormones which drive sexuality. The female pattern became a male pattern. If, however, the same injection of testosterone was given when the animal was twenty days old, it had no effect. Thus, like the sweat glands of humans, there is a critical, sensitive period in which the animal's sexual physiology is plastic and can be permanently changed. After that period plasticity is lost.

The concept of sensitive periods in early life has long been familiar to biologists who study animal behaviour. Konrad Lorenz showed that newly hatched goslings could be made to behave as if their mother was a dog – if the first moving object they saw after hatching was a dog. Long ago Pliny described 'a goose which followed Lacydes as faithfully as a dog' and Reginald of Durham wrote of eider ducks which followed humans because humans were the first living creatures they saw after hatching.

SLOWING GROWTH

If a baby in the womb becomes undernourished its immediate response is to use its own stores of food for the energy it needs to continue to grow. It can also alter the food it uses for energy – use protein instead of sugar, for example. If, however, it continues to be undernourished its rate of growth will slow. This may be due simply to the constraint on growth imposed by less food, but it is also adaptive because it enhances the baby's ability to survive by reducing the amount of energy it needs. If its growth depended only on genetic commands issued at conception it might outstrip its nutrient supply and perish. If adequate nutrition is restored after a few days, the baby resumes growth at the previous rate, but prolonged undernutrition may slow growth irreversibly.

We use the word 'adaptation' to describe the changes by which living things surmount the challenges of life. People sometimes talk about growth and development as though they are unalterable consequences of genetic inheritance. 'John is intelligent and growing tall just like his father'. True, perhaps, but John

may not have become so intelligent in less stimulating surroundings and his growth will slow if he is undernourished, ill or
stressed in other ways. Development and growth are not commanded by a single blueprint; they are dynamic processes with
improvisations and elaborations that depend on circumstances.
They show a subtle balance between inflexibility and flexibility.
Once cells are set on course to become muscle or liver it is
difficult to persuade them to become something intermediate.
But within these lanes of development there is flexibility, more
muscle or less muscle, different mixtures of the various specialised
cells which form the liver.

Whether the responses of an animal during development are
adaptive, helping it to survive, or simply the result of constraint
are recurring themes. Biologists have always been fascinated by
the way animals cope with life in a temporary pond: shrimps, tadpoles, beetles, larvae, packed into a space smaller than your living
room. One day it disappears. Some of the creatures disappear
with it and the species has to recolonise it again when it refills.
Others lay eggs in the mud or burrow into it themselves and wait
for the pond to refill. The tadpoles speed up their development,
grow legs and hop away as frogs. A clever trick that allows the
tadpoles to survive? Or simply a mechanical response to less food
or warmer water? Given that the tadpole's response is obviously
beneficial it looks like a clever trick, and the balance of evidence
favours this interpretation.

Mechanically the trick could work in two ways: either changing water temperature or chemical content could have a direct
effect on the genes and the proteins they produce, or the central
control mechanisms may change. The term 'metamorphosis' is
used to describe the orchestrated progression from frogspawn, to
tadpole, to a frog able to climb out of its pond and live on land.
The conductor of this metamorphic orchestra, coordinating
the diverse changes in each tissue through to the climax of life
on land, is a hormonal messenger produced by the thyroid
gland. This hormone appears in the blood at an early stage
and the amount continues to rise until the climax. It controls
metamorphosis by regulating the 'expression of genes', that is,

the production of the particular protein that the gene is coded to make. While the thyroid hormone conducts, another hormonal messenger is in the wings, waiting to respond should stressful situations arise. Production of cortisol is one of the main stress responses in humans and higher animals. Stress responses prepare animals for 'fight or flight' in the face of predators, famine and fire. They are controlled by part of the brain, the hypothalamus, which acts as an interface between the external and internal environments, and controls a variety of processes from reproduction to metabolism. During development the stress hormones speed up maturation. The tadpole in the drying pond has a surge of cortisol and hops away. The stressed human baby has a surge of cortisol that matures its lungs and prepares it for an early birth. This is discussed in more detail in Chapter 4.

The baby establishes a trajectory of growth, a path that will lead it to a target body size at birth, at an early stage, possibly within a few days after conception, even perhaps before the fertilised egg has reached the womb. Having established a trajectory, it tries to sustain this throughout its time in the womb. After birth, the infant resets the trajectory, and after a while growth sets off on a new path and tempo. The rate of growth that is established in early pregnancy is important because it determines the demand for food in later gestation, when the baby's food requirements are greatest and when the placenta is beginning to fail. A baby that is large at any point in time needs more food, and so does a baby that is growing fast. If a mother is not adequately nourished, her baby is more likely to have to slow its growth if it is growing rapidly. The baby boy is more vulnerable to undernutrition than the baby girl because he grows faster. This is a general phenomenon affecting mammals and birds, lambs and blackbirds, and we shall return to it.

TRADE-OFFS

Because a baby is plastic it is able to respond to undernutrition. One of its responses is to slow its growth. Why should this or other responses to undernutrition lead to disease in later life?

Given that it is not possible for most of the key organs of the body to recuperate or restore themselves after birth, because they are already complete, why cannot the baby simply remain small, with fewer cells, and lead a normal life?

One possible answer is that it may run out of key cells as they begin to be lost through ageing: the ageing lion's teeth fall out; it cannot feed; it dies. But this is too simple. The Japanese have small babies but have among the longest lifespans in the world. Heart disease was almost unknown a hundred years ago; something must have changed. Perhaps the inner environment that is established in an undernourished baby, an environment in which nutrients are handled thriftily, becomes a liability if food becomes abundant. The 'thrifty phenotype' has now established itself as a potentially important explanation of the modern epidemic of diabetes. It incorporates the fundamental biological idea shown by the sweat glands.

Another fundamental of biology is the occurrence of 'trade-offs'. On any day of the week in the maternity hospitals of the Western world, babies may be seen sacrificing the growth of one body part for the benefit of another. A baby receiving an inadequate supply of nutrients or oxygen may protect its brain by diverting to it more of the blood returning from the placenta. It does this by a simple mammalian trick, which was discovered by scientists studying baby seals. To meet the challenge of surviving long periods when the mother is underwater and oxygen becomes scarce, the baby seal in the womb shuts down the supply of blood to all the organs of the body except the brain and heart. Thus, by 'brain-sparing' it survives until the mother surfaces. The diversion of blood away from the body to the brain is accomplished by shunting blood through an aperture between the right and left sides of the heart. Human babies do the same. At birth the aperture closes and shunting is no longer possible. The human brain is large and protecting it in times of scarcity has exaggerated costs for other parts of the body, notably the liver which is large in a baby, but also other organs such as the lung and the kidney. Protecting them is not an immediate priority as, until birth, the mother performs many of their functions on the baby's behalf.

And so in the ultrasound room, doctors regularly see babies diverting blood away from their bodies. The circumference of the brain and abdomen are measured and if the brain continues to grow at the expense of the liver the time has come to consider inducing the delivery of the baby, to give it a new source of food and put an end to the trading-off between brain and liver.

The existence of mechanisms by which the growth of an organ such as the brain can be protected at the expense of other organs reflects the different priorities accorded to the growth of different parts of the body. Bones, or at least some bones, seem to have high priorities. More than two thousand years ago Xenophon, the Athenian warlord, observed that the size of a foal's shin bone at birth could be used to predict the final size of the horse. Muscle and fat have lower priorities, but ballet teachers can identify likely pupils at an early age.

Caddis flies provide an interesting example of the general phenomenon of trading-off. Their larvae live in fresh water. When they change into pupae, and thereafter adult flies, they do not feed. The flies must therefore live off their food stores, the 'capital' acquired by the larvae. The fly's body has two main parts – an abdomen, which consists almost entirely of the reproductive system – and a chest, which comprises the wings. During pupal life food from the stores is allocated to both. Thereafter body shape is fixed. If food is scarce because the stores are small, to which body part should it be allocated – should reproduction be favoured at the expense of flight or vice versa?

The answer, like that to many questions in biology, is that it depends on the circumstances. Caddis fly larvae defend themselves from fish and other predators by building a strong case around their bodies. The case is made of sand, held together by silk, which the larvae make. If larvae are removed from their cases they rebuild them, the need for defence overriding other priorities. This diverts nutrients to the production of silk and away from the food stores, which the larvae are accumulating. One species of caddis fly larva is a scavenger living in streams. The eggs hatch in the autumn, and a long ten-month period of larval development through winter and spring is followed by a brief adult life in the summer. Adults emerge from the pupae, mate and die within only a few days. In contrast, another species of caddis fly is herbivorous and lives in temporary ponds, which dry up in summer. It has a shorter period of larval life than the stream dweller. It has, however, a much longer adult life, lasting four months, as it has to survive until the ponds refill.

In both these species, when larvae have to divert energy into rebuilding their cases the size of the adults is reduced. The adult stream dwellers, however, preserve their abdomens and hence their capacity to reproduce, at the expense of their chests and their capacity to fly. The pond dwellers do the reverse. Preserving the ability to fly is unimportant to the stream dweller for whom the imperative is to reproduce in the brief period of its adult life. The pond dweller, however, has to survive through the summer until winter rains replenish the ponds in which it breeds. Thus the caddis fly, when depleted of resources at pupation, does not alter its body form in a fixed way. Rather, the way in which adult body form is altered is flexible.

LIFE HISTORY THEORY

The trading-off of body parts by the baby and the caddis fly are examples of a phenomenon that is encapsulated in so-called 'life history theory' and applies to humans in the same way as it does to other animals. Life history theory states that, if the total amount of energy available to an animal is limited, as it usually is, increased allocation of energy to one trait, such as growth, must reduce allocation to one or more other traits, such as repair of the body. The lizards in Brittany grew faster than those in the southern mountains of France, but they lived shorter lives. They had to trade off the advantages of rapid growth and early reproduction against the disadvantages of a shorter life. Reproducing at an earlier age is a biological gain, because it reduces the likelihood of death before reproduction and thereby increases the likelihood of passing genes to the next generation. An ideal creature would reproduce immediately after birth, produce large numbers of large offspring and repeat this through a long life-span. It would also outnumber its competitors, escape from its predators and catch prey easily. This is not possible. The needs of one activity conflict with those of another. The activities required to avoid predators differ from those which catch prey. There must be trade-offs in which the benefits of increasing one activity are set against its disadvantages.

If you doubt that the laws that govern lizards govern man, look around. Has not the abundant food of recent generations brought more rapid growth and earlier sexual maturation? A hundred years ago Finnish girls began to menstruate at around sixteen years of age; many did not menstruate until they were twenty. Today they begin at thirteen, many begin at eleven. In one brief century Finland made the move from the southern mountains of France to Brittany.

There are many reasons why humans and other animals face food shortage during development. Poor food, overcrowding, bad weather and other hostile influences that arise periodically lead to large differences in the environments which members of the same species experience during development. They may be born late in the breeding season, when worsening conditions reduce food supply; or their parents may fail to make adequate provision for them. Animals with a prolonged egg stage have a 'capital' development strategy: unlike the human baby, they have no daily 'income' of food. Reptiles and many birds hatch from their eggs with their bodies close to their final form: they are therefore more vulnerable to lack of nutritional 'capital' than insects, which are hatched as larvae and have opportunities to compensate for lack of food before they reach their adult form. A butterfly lays its eggs on the lushest vegetation so that the caterpillars have the best start in life.

For the human baby, as for all living things during development, resources available are insufficient to perfect every structure, every function. One is traded off against another. If resources are reduced, trade-offs must be more intensive. Is this why small babies get more heart disease?

In Hertfordshire we found that there was progressively less

heart disease across the whole range of birthweight. An interpretation of this is that there are graded trade-offs across the range of human growth in the womb, and between the smaller and larger baby there is a gradual reduction in the extent of trading-off. In development, however, there may be switches as well as graded responses. Both Darwin and Wallace were impressed with the shapes and extraordinary variability in the horns of male beetles. Within a single population of the same species the horns range from a tiny knob to structures longer than the entire male body. Darwin thought they were mere ornaments whose purpose was to attract females. We now know, however, that they are weapons, used when males fight each other to gain access to females. The largest beetles have the longest horns, and body size is strongly influenced by the amount of food available to the larvae. Are long horns simply an extravagance open only to the better-nourished animals? It seems that they are. Experiments on the dung beetle show that increasing amounts of food do not result in progressively longer and longer horns. Rather, there is a threshold of feeding below which the beetle has no horns and above which it has fully developed horns. This implies the existence of a developmental switch that gives an abrupt response to changing food intake. Switches are common during development and depend on central control mechanisms acting through hormones.

BABIES' SHAPES

Although it is simple and convenient to measure, birthweight is a poor summary of the dynamic process of foetal growth and does not capture the effects of undernutrition on the development of particular tissues. The weight of a turkey is useful to the cook; the weight of a baby provides an inadequate description of its growth, just as your weight is an inadequate description of your physique. Different paths of growth, such as rapid early growth followed by slowing, or a moderate rate of growth maintained throughout gestation, give rise to babies with the same birthweights. Chapter 2 described how midwives in Preston and

Sheffield made other measurements, including the baby's length, and the circumferences of its head, arms, chest and abdomen. Because different parts of the body have phases of rapid growth at different times during development, the proportions of these measurements to each other give an insight into the path and tempo of growth in the womb. A baby with a large head in relation to its body has maintained brain growth, which begins early in pregnancy, but has been unable to sustain growth of its trunk later on. A thin baby may have failed to make adequate muscle, which has a 'critical' period of growth in late pregnancy, or it may have been unable to accumulate fat, which increases rapidly in late pregnancy to provide a food store after birth, when the baby has to learn a new method of feeding. Though they may have the same birthweights, babies that are thin or short in relation to the size of their heads have followed different paths of growth. Because of this their future health will be different.

Studies in animals have shown that different paths of growth in the womb may lead to babies that, though having the same overall body size at birth, as measured by birthweight, are different in the relative size of their organs. The importance of this to the subsequent health of the baby will be discussed later. Meanwhile, it emphasises how birthweight provides only the crudest of summary measures of the day-to-day adaptations, constraints and trade-offs, triumphs and failures of the previous nine months. Despite these limitations birthweight is a strong predictor of heart disease. The processes that link early growth with health in later life must be powerful ones.

Persisting undernutrition sustained from early on in gestation leads to proportional failure of growth in head size and length. At birth the baby is miniature. Many Chinese babies are like this. Undernutrition that begins in mid or late pregnancy leads to disproportionate growth, reflected in thinness or shortness at birth. Many Indian babies are thin or short. The World Health Organisation compared newborn babies in China, India and Sweden. The Chinese babies had an average weight of more than 7 pounds (3.2 kg), but they had smaller heads and shorter bodies than the Indian babies, who weighed only 6½ pounds (2.9

kg) because they were thin. The Swedish babies weighed more than 8 pounds (3.6 kg), and had the largest heads and the longest bodies. The Chinese babies, although the least successful in terms of brain and body growth, were fatter than the Swedish babies. In this way birthweight conceals important differences between babies. The different body shapes of newborn babies reflect the food they received at different stages of gestation. Thinness and stunting among newborn babies are not a thing of the past in Western countries. A quarter of all baby boys born in Britain today are recognisably thin.

BOYS ARE MORE VULNERABLE

In Hertfordshire, as in the Western world generally, heart disease is more common among men. Those who subscribe to the view that heart disease is primarily the result of lifestyle explain this by the more reckless, cavalier lifestyles of men, and their predisposition to smoke, drink and overeat, given half a chance. It used to be thought that women were also protected by their oestrogens, but this now seems unlikely. If heart disease originates during development, why should men be more vulnerable than women?

Shortage of food during development may not bear equally on the two sexes. The faster growing sex, the boy in humans, is more vulnerable. Generally in mammals if mothers are in poor condition, their male children are more severely affected. In humans more sons than daughters die in the womb and during childhood. In mammals and among those birds in which the two sexes have different body size, males grow faster and for longer than females, and need more food. Among sheep, young rams eat 15 per cent more food than ewes of the same age. In the nest young male blackbirds eat 30 per cent more food than young females. Males are therefore more vulnerable in times of food scarcity. The advantage of large body size when males compete with each other to reproduce are offset by the greater risk of death when food is short.

The success of male animals in reproducing is often more

variable than females. Some males have many partners, many children; others have none. The future reproductive success of a young male may be more readily jeopardised by poor conditions than the success of a female. Among red deer on the island of Rum, Scotland, low birthweight reduced the later reproductive success of males, as measured by the number of their offspring, but not that of females. In Hertfordshire men who were small at birth are less likely to marry: around 20 per cent of men who weighed 5½ pounds (2.5 kg) or less at birth remain unmarried in middle age compared with only 5 per cent in men weighing 7¾ pounds (3.5 kg) or more. This is not simply the result of men who were larger at birth being taller as adults and hence more attractive to women. At any given height, those who were smaller at birth are less likely to marry. It seems that restriction of growth before birth alters some aspects of partner selection – sexuality, socialisation, personality or emotional responses. Is the small baby forced to trade these off? Do you still believe that humans are not like other animals?

It is folklore that strong, dominant women tend to produce sons. Among other animals, for mothers in poor condition investment in daughters may be a better option than investment in sons. On the other hand, for mothers in good condition, investment in sons is a better option because, on average, they will produce more progeny than daughters. If the food of female hamsters is restricted after they are born they will tend to produce more daughters than sons, irrespective of how they are fed during pregnancy. Their daughters seem to experience stress during development because they in turn tend to produce more daughters than sons even if they are well fed after birth. Inter-generational effects of this kind have been little studied in humans. We know remarkably little about how the nutrition of a girl will affect her later reproduction; but it is certain that it can. We return to this in Chapter 5.

Meanwhile if sheep, blackbirds, red deer and hamsters seem to you interesting but remote from human pregnancy with its antenatal clinics and labour wards, consider this. For more than a century government statisticians in Britain have commented on the changing proportion of boys and girls born in Britain. While young men died in their thousands in the trenches in the First World War, the proportion of boys being born increased. Was it nature's way of replenishing the dwindling numbers of males? How did it work? One recent theory, based on the different viability of sperm carrying male or female chromosomes, proposed that periods of intense and repeated sexual intercourse – as might occur when a soldier returned home on leave – were more likely to favour sperm carrying male chromosomes. We do not know the answer, but we do know that in deer and in humans, mothers in good condition tend to invest in males and that adverse conditions in pregnancy are related to a reduced proportion of boys being born. Whether your baby is a boy or a girl is only in part a random event, for human pregnancy is governed by the same laws that govern other animals. The human mother provides the arena for biological processes we little understand. Once they have begun we cannot control them and we interfere with them at our peril.

THE UNDERNOURISHED INFANT

After birth a baby responds differently to undernutrition. No longer receiving food and oxygen through blood returning from the placenta, it has readjusted its circulation so that it can receive food through its intestines and oxygen through its lungs. The capacity to protect the brain by diverting blood away from the body is greatly reduced. Much of the body is complete. Organs like the kidney, tissues like muscle, are beyond their critical periods of development and are no longer vulnerable. Two large organs, the brain and the liver, remain plastic and therefore can be permanently changed. The liver has had to change its functions. Hitherto it has been the first organ to receive and process the protein and sugars coming from the mother. In the womb the placenta and liver conduct an intimate dialogue. After birth the baby's diet changes. It receives food intermittently instead of constantly. High concentrations of cholesterol and saturated fat – the now forbidden foods of the Western world – are taken into the body from the mother's milk and carried in the blood from the infant's intestines to the liver, where they are broken down and re-formed.

Insulin regulated growth in the womb and continues to control it after birth, until around one year of age. During this time the baby continues to grow rapidly, and its growth will slow in response to poor nutrition, illness, poor living conditions or stress. In the womb and during infancy nutrition has its strongest direct effect on body size. The height of a child at two years of age can be used to predict its final adult height, just as the shin bone of a newborn foal predicts the size of the horse. After age two years a child's height tends to 'track' in the same way as blood pressure and blood cholesterol.

WHY DOES PLASTICITY CEASE?

Living things are plastic during development, but this plasticity is ultimately lost. For the different tissues and systems of the body there are critical periods of development during which they are plastic and sensitive to the environment. After that plasticity is lost and functional capacity becomes fixed. When the sensitive period is over the effects of the environment have become 'hard-wired' in the body, preserved for a lifetime.

Biologists discuss why plasticity is not retained throughout the lifetime of an individual. To be able to change the structure of our bodies to match changes in the environment, to meet famine or plenty, cold or heat, would seem to be the pinnacle of evolution. When soldiers fight hand to hand, tall, strong men are favoured; when captured and poorly fed the tall men die first, because they need more food and this requirement cannot be changed. When former British prisoners of the Japanese reunited after the Second World War their short stature, compared with that of other soldiers, was remarked on. So why can't we remain plastic?

One possibility is that there may be a tension between genetic variation and plasticity. If each genotype could give rise to a very large number of phenotypes that change through life as conditions change, there might be insufficient variation in the genes within a species to allow the species to evolve and make major changes in the long term. Alternatively, the costs of remaining plastic may be too high. Plasticity requires maintenance of machinery that senses the environment and regulates the body's responses to it. In order to obtain information about the environment, the individual may have to expend energy and reduce other activities such as finding food or expose itself to danger. Environmental cues may be unreliable and lead to mistakes, a mismatch between the body and its environment.

Whatever the resolution of this question, it is clear that humans are no exception to a general theme of nature. Individuals in their lives are highly sensitive to the environment while they develop. But once developed, their form and function are fixed; their bodies are governed by their own control machinery and their sensitivity to the environment is reduced. In the search for the environmental causes of disease in adult life, the period of development is a logical starting point.

4

The Undernourished Baby

Before proceeding to examine biological processes which, in combination with the prosperity factor, carry the undernourished baby to disease and premature death, two other subjects need to be addressed. The first is the placenta, the gateway between mother and baby, whose function importantly determines the baby's nutrition, and whose weight had been faithfully recorded, year after year, by the midwives of Preston and Sheffield. It is unclear why they did so, since the purpose of pregnancy is to produce a baby not a placenta; but, as it turned out, it was marvellous that they did. The second subject needing to be addressed is the nature of the prosperity factor, which leads to rising epidemics of heart disease as nations become more prosperous.

THAT WONDERFUL ORGAN

Among mammals the placenta, by which the baby is attached to the uterus, shows more diversity than any other organ. While the placentas of pigs and sheep have four layers of cells which separate the bloodstreams of mother and baby, the human placenta has only two. Because of this intimate contact food passes more readily from the mother to the baby: this, it is thought, allows the human brain to develop to an advanced state before birth. The placenta has three main functions: it is the gate between mother and baby, transferring food from the mother and waste from the baby; it makes hormones, which signal to the mother the continuing presence of the baby, while other hormones mobilise fats and sugar from the mother's blood stores; and it protects the baby from the mother's immune system, which could attack the baby, because it is 'foreign' to the mother's body, half of its genes coming from the father. The effect of poor nutrition on the human placenta has been a source of concern for a long while. In 1884 the *Encyclopaedia Britannica* commented that 'the building of the placenta by the mother and the performance of the function of that wonderful organ requires certain favouring conditions. These are certainly not to be found in factory labour.'

In mid-pregnancy the placenta grows faster than the baby; thereafter it loses its priority and grows more slowly. The larger the placenta grows, the more food will be transferred to the baby. Therefore the weight of the placenta at birth correlates with the weight of the baby, though the correlation is not necessarily very close because 'amount' and 'efficiency of function' do not exactly tally. Our studies in Preston showed, wholly unexpectedly, that people whose birthweights had been lower than would be expected from the weights of their placentas had considerably higher blood pressures fifty years later, and more were being treated for hypertension. Little was known about what might cause a disparity between the size of the baby and the size of its placenta. We published this surprising finding in the *British Medical Journal*, pointing out that the babies whose birthweights were relatively low in relation to the weight of their placentas were characterised by having relatively large heads in relation to the size of their bodies. They had, we suggested, diverted blood to protect their brains in the way described in the last chapter. We further suggested, on the basis of our maps, that the prevention of high blood pressure might depend more on improving the nutrition of mothers and their babies than on persuading middle-aged men and women to eat less salt. We awaited a thunderbolt.

The orthodox views of the causes of heart disease are protected in gladiatorial style, not by the thoughtful exchanges that characterise many other areas of science. The slimmest of justifications for this behaviour is in the writings of Karl Popper, for whom the process of science required that new ideas were subjected to intensive attacks to disprove them. This is but one view. Thomas Kuhn had other views and described how, for simple human reasons related to status and reputation, scientists become locked into paradigms from which it proves difficult to escape without loss of status. Medical research is a practical subject; we are not questing new laws of the universe. Speke discovered the source of the Nile, Burton did not believe him. Instead of clever debates and acerbic articles in their journal *The Nile Explorer*, the doubters should have raised an expedition and gone and found the real source of the Nile. If people disbelieved that raised blood pressure was linked to the baby's nutrition, the main obligation is to find out what does cause raised blood pressure and not devote their time to writing acrimonious letters.

On this occasion we did not receive any. Instead, a letter of invitation came from the research group in Adelaide, Australia, who study foetal growth. They are among the foremost groups of foetal physiologists who, in Australia, New Zealand, the USA and Europe, made common cause with us at an early stage of our research. To those who study the growth and development of babies, the proposition that poor nutrition in the womb might lead to heart disease and diabetes in later life was wholly unre-markable.

In Australia I was told that shepherds have known for a long time that if, after mating, ewes are moved on to poor pasture – the pasture on the hillside rather than the pasture in the valley – for a month or so before being returned to rich pasture, the lamb will be bigger than if the ewe remained on rich pasture throughout pregnancy. This runs counter to common sense. Surely a lamb will do better if its mother is well fed throughout pregnancy? Recently Australian scientists have discovered how it works: when a foetal lamb is undernourished it increases the size of its placenta to obtain more food from the mother, enlarging the gate. When in later pregnancy the ewe returns to rich pasture this enlarged gate allows more food to be transferred to the lamb than would otherwise have been the case. Mammals are like plants, which grow in different ways if they are well or badly nourished. Plants on good soil invest more of their resources in leaves and less in roots, so that they can use the increased energy obtained from more leaves to grow rapidly. Those on poor soil invest in roots, in order to survive. Human babies whose mothers are anaemic – a common occurrence even in the Western world – receive less oxygen, which is carried in the mothers' blood to the placenta. They respond by increasing the size of the placentas, to extract more oxygen.

When the undernourished lamb or the oxygen-deprived baby invest in their placenta they have to pay a cost. The increased mass of the placenta requires more energy to sustain it. If there is insufficient energy to supply the needs of both placenta and foetus, foetal growth may have to be sacrificed. The foetus may have to divert blood to protect its brain or it may become thin and wasted; the placenta has to be preserved at all costs. The lamb is only able to enlarge its placenta if the ewe was mature and in good condition at the time of conception. If she was immature or in poor condition, later undernutrition will slow the growth of both the placenta and the baby. Thus at an early stage of our research we were made aware that we should not expect constancy. These remarkable observations in sheep suggested that a baby's responses to undernutrition may depend on the mother's condition at the time of conception.

GROWTH IN CHILDHOOD

A new insight into how the effects of prosperity might add to those of poor growth in the womb and during infancy, and lead to heart disease, came when we looked at the childhood growth of people who later developed heart disease and diabetes. Studies by other groups in the USA and Europe showed that among children and adults the highest blood pressures and the highest blood sugars were found in those who were small at birth but were now overweight. A study in Caerphilly, Wales, where the health of a group of men had been studied for many years, similarly showed that low birthweight had a much greater impact on heart disease in men who were overweight. Not grossly over-weight, for unlike diabetes the risk of heart disease is not greatly increased by being overweight.

This raised a number of questions. Did low birthweight make much difference? Was the main cause of heart disease and diabetes becoming fat in middle life? Was it, as one paper was wittily entitled, 'Barker or Burger'? A more profound question was whether the path of growth that led to being overweight was important. Did it matter whether a person first became over-weight in childhood, adolescence or middle age? Was it the path and tempo of weight gain rather than simply being overweight? In general, heavier babies tend to become fatter adults than lighter ones, but people developing heart disease and diabetes were more overweight than would have been expected from their birthweight.

In a study based on the maternity records kept for many years in Uppsala, Sweden, the highest blood pressure levels were found among men who had been small at birth but had grown tall as adults, rather than becoming overweight. One suggested explanation was that the tall men had experienced in the womb a greater suppression of their genetically determined growth potential than short men with the same birthweight. Such an explanation presupposes that the rate at which a baby grows is commanded by its genes, an issue discussed in later chapters, but these observations in Uppsala again pointed to the importance of studying how people with heart disease, diabetes or hypertension grew as children.

Although Margaret Burnside's nurses continued to visit the children of Hertfordshire until they reached school age at five years, they did not measure their heights and weights, though they recorded their illnesses, which still bear on their health today. Children who had one or more attacks of pneumonia or bron-chitis are today, as elderly people, more likely to have chronic bronchitis and suffer from a persistent cough and shortness of breath. Their lungs were lastingly damaged by their childhood illness. The need to find records of the growth of individual children fifty and more years ago led to further searches of Britain's archives and records offices. Studying childhood growth was an important scientific activity fifty years ago and the records of some of the studies survived, but they were on too small a scale, just a few hundred children. Children's heights and weights were often measured when they were at school, but in Britain this was done on only one or two occasions and the records were usually destroyed. The search in Britain came to an end.

A chance encounter in Brussels, and a beer in the airport bar, led to the discovery of what may prove to be the world's most detailed set of records of the growth, illnesses and living conditions of a large group of men and women who are now approaching old age. From early in the last century the size of all babies born in the Helsinki University Central Hospital, Finland, was measured in the same detailed way as in Sheffield. Child welfare clinics were established in the city in 1934, and recorded growth between birth and school age. When the children reached school their growth continued to be recorded by two school doctors who visited each child at school in the city every six months.

The realisation that disease originates during early life had added to modern epidemiology an archaeological dimension. To understand the present we needed to know the past. To know the past we needed to have the heights and weights of large numbers of children, measured at intervals as they grew up, accurately recorded and carefully preserved. When our colleagues in the Helsinki Institute of Public Health showed us into the city archives and we saw row upon row of meticulous records going back for a hundred years, it was a rare moment. If Hertfordshire had opened the Tomb of Tutankhamun, we were now entering the chamber.

By further good fortune, Finland had introduced a unique personal identification for all its citizens in 1971. For the purposes of research, this number can be used to determine whether a person is alive or dead, what they died of, whether they have ever been admitted to hospital and if so, with what illness, and whether they are taking medicines for chronic disease. Over the next five years a group at the Institute painstakingly computerised the information and linked it to other information on the people's lives and illnesses. Came the day in 1998 when more than 8000 people had been documented. For each individual there were on average eighteen measurements of height and weight from birth to twelve years of age. For the first time we would see whether people who developed coronary heart disease and diabetes in adult life grew differently from other people as children.

And they did. The Finnish boys and girls who later developed heart disease grew more slowly in the womb than did the other children among whom they lived. The boys also grew more slowly during infancy. The same findings as in Hertfordshire. Thereafter, however, both the boys and girls began to put on weight at a greater rate than other children, though this was not matched by similar rapid growth in height. It was as though the children, having been small, short or thin at birth tried to 'catch up' with the others by putting on weight rapidly. The path of growth of children who went on to receive treatment for diabetes was similarly characterised by an initial phase of slow growth followed by a phase of rapid weight gain. Whereas, however, the weights of children who later developed heart disease caught up with the average for all the children, those who developed diabetes caught up and then continued gaining weight at the same speed. It was as though these children, having fallen behind in a running race, not only caught up but raced through the pack and ended up ahead.

Though there were interesting differences in detail between the growth of boys and girls who later developed heart disease or diabetes, the general picture was the same – restriction of growth followed by rapid gain in weight. That the gain in weight was not matched by corresponding gain in height was not surprising since it was already known that heart disease was more common among shorter people. But when we looked at the path of growth that led to hypertension, we saw what the researchers in Uppsala had seen: rapid gain in height as well as weight.

Chapter 8 returns to 'catch up' or 'compensatory' growth and why it may lead to disease. Because children are only able to catch up if food is plentiful, small babies and infants in the Third World tended, until recently, to remain small as children. Compensatory growth is a Western phenomenon. We concluded that we had found a prosperity factor, and that the origins of heart disease and diabetes lay in undernutrition in the womb and during infancy, followed by compensatory weight gain thereafter.

UNDERNUTRITION AND LATER DISEASE

Though much is known about the early growth of domestic animals, little is known about the long-term destiny of those whose growth is impaired. We do not know whether runt pigs age more rapidly, because their lives are brought to an end long before they reach old age. Until recently we have known little about the destiny of small babies. Over the years, they become dispersed among other children and are lost from sight. Only now, with the emergence of new kinds of epidemiological study, in which people are traced from birth to death, are we beginning to see the large impact of early growth and development on later disease. It has proved difficult for some social scientists to accept that, when a child that has had inadequate or imbalanced nutrition in early life is moved to a good home and is well fed, the biological legacy of its early experiences persists. It seems discouraging; but the reverse also holds. Biological advantages acquired by good experiences in early life persist despite later adversity. A good start is a gift that lasts for a lifetime.

That inadequate feeding in early life is associated with chronic disease in later life, after reproduction is complete, is in one sense unsurprising. Life history theory, discussed in Chapter 3, states that when the energy available to a living thing is limited, as it usually is, there are trade-offs. One activity – growth for example – is achieved at the expense of another, repair of the body and longevity, for instance. The less energy there is the more trade-offs there are. It is far from clear in humans under what circumstances the trade-offs include reduced lifespan. Small Japanese babies live long lives: small Indian babies die young. Fortunately, this profound and interesting question can be left unanswered as we learn more about the actual processes which are initiated in early life and lead to later disease. In this we doctors have an advantage over those who study domestic animals and whose knowledge of nutrition so greatly exceeds ours. Whereas the farmer is not interested in the lifespan of the runt pig, and even less interested in what it may die from, ageing and the diseases it brings are a focus of medical research.

HIGH BLOOD PRESSURE

People in the town of Framingham, Massachusetts, have been studied for forty years or more. This famous study was among the first to show that raised blood pressure increases the risk of coronary heart disease and stroke. The first suggestions that low birthweight was linked to raised blood pressure came from studies of a group of Swedish military recruits, and from men and women in Britain who were all born during the same week in 1946, and whose social development, behaviour, illnesses and growth have been repeatedly studied since then. Later studies showed that the link was detectable in childhood, and its existence has now been confirmed in large numbers of studies around the world. As has been described, a person's blood pressure 'tracks' through childhood, suggesting that at least some of the processes which regulate it become set early in life. That this setting should occur in the womb is perhaps unsurprising because much of our internal environment is established at that time. The pressure and flow of blood in a baby's circulation are critically important because its nutrition depends on its maintaining an adequate blood flow through the placenta.

At a fair a palmist looks at your hand and tells your fortune. She may examine the shape of your hand, the lines on your palm, your fingerprints. It is entertaining; there is also a rational basis for it. The hands are formed early in gestation. The fingerprints are established before the nineteenth week. At birth undernourished babies tend to have 'whorls', complex patterns of ridges that are thought to result from the fingers being swollen when the skin is first laid down. People with more whorls tend to have higher blood pressure than people with fewer. Undernourished babies that are short tend to have narrow palms. People with narrow palms tend to have high blood pressure. The palmist examining your hand is being informed about events during your life in the womb, and these events have contributed, among other things, to the level of your blood pressure today and to your health tomorrow.

There are interesting inconsistencies between the many studies of the link between small size at birth and later blood pressure. In some of them, blood pressure is higher in people who were thin at birth; in others it is higher in those who were short, or had a small body in relation to their head size. In some studies blood pressure is linked to a small placenta, in others to a disproportionately large placenta and in others it is not linked to placental size at all. Each of these birth phenotypes can be regarded as the result of foetal undernutrition, but the inconsistencies have led to criticism. This criticism reflects the frustration of statisticians who maintain that what is true should be consistent, that one human being is much the same as another, and that truth is reached by adding the findings on large numbers of them, preferably very large numbers, together. Every doctor knows, however, that patients respond differently to treatment. Doctors and biologists live with heterogeneity. We see that a single event can have many different consequences depending on the individual to whom it occurs. Babies respond differently to undernutrition, depending on its timing, intensity and nature, and on the speed at which the baby is growing. The question to be answered is whether these different responses result in people whose blood pressures are raised because different parts of the internal environment which regulate blood pressure have been reset. If so, they may need different treatment if they develop hypertension in later life. Blood pressure is regulated by the kidney, by the elasticity of the arteries, by hormones such as cortisol and by the nervous system. Drugs for hypertension act in various parts of this system.

People who had low birthweight are at twice the risk of needing drugs to control their blood pressures in later life. Yet until middle age or later, the blood pressures of people who were small at birth or had altered placental growth are, in most studies, only a little higher than those of other people, insufficiently raised to be a source of concern to themselves or their doctors. It is known that if one part of the system that regulates blood pressure is damaged, the other parts of the system are able to compensate for many years. If you lost a kidney in an accident or donated it to a relative your blood pressure would be little changed. Constancy of the internal environment has to be maintained. But eventually, as the system begins to wear out with age, this becomes impossible and blood pressure begins to rise. When blood pressure rises it damages the control system and the gentle rise in pressure that accompanies normal ageing becomes a steep rise, a climbing pathway that leads to hypertension and the need for treatment.

A kidney comprises up to a million identical functional units called nephrons, through which blood circulates so that waste is extracted and urine formed. People who had low birthweight have up to three times fewer nephrons as people who were large at birth. The kidney may not have high priority for growth in a baby because, before birth, the excretion of waste is carried out through the placenta and into the mother. If there are fewer nephrons in a kidney, each will receive more blood. This seems to increase the wear and tear on them, and hasten the death of nephrons that occurs with normal ageing. As nephrons continue to die, blood pressure climbs. This itself accelerates further nephron death and, it is thought, sets in motion a self-perpetuating cycle of rising blood pressure and nephron loss.

When the results of kidney transplantation across the USA were analysed it was found that the worst results, with failure of the transplanted kidney after only a few months or years, occurred when the kidney from a small person was transplanted into a large muscular man. Again each nephron received too much blood, was damaged by it and hastened to an early death. Could this explain why the path to hypertension in the Swedish and Finnish studies is small size at birth and rapid growth thereafter?

Out of all the states in the USA the highest rates of kidney failure occur in South Carolina, in the Deep South. Kidney failure is common there; it is usually preceded by hypertension or diabetes, but there are other causes. More men than women are affected, people as young as twenty get it, many are poor, and the main burden falls on Americans of African descent, among whom it is five times more common than it is among whites. We know all this because the costs of treatment, whether dialysis or transplant, are borne by the Federal Government and they keep careful accounts of where they spend. South Carolina is part of the stroke belt, the cluster of states in the Deep South with high rates of stroke. Chapter 1 described how this could be related to its long period of impoverishment after the Civil War and the continuing poor growth of babies, reflected in their high death rates around the time of birth. A possible explanation for the high rates of kidney failure in the state, as a result of a variety of different diseases, is that it reflects the limited reserves of kidney cells in people who were born small but grew tall. Where in the world, my colleagues in Charleston suggested, could this be happening on a grander scale than in their state? By yet another piece of the good fortune that has attended our research, every baby born in the state since 1950 has had its birthweight recorded on its birth certificate – something that has never occurred in Britain. It was therefore relatively simple, at least in principle and when viewed from the British side of the Atlantic, to find out the birthweights of people with kidney failure and show that, as a group, they had lower birthweights. The paper that described these findings was published in a prominent American medical journal and suggested the Federal Government might offset the spiralling costs of treating people with kidney failure by investing more in protecting the nutrition and health of girls and young women.

The kidney story is but one explanation for the origins of high blood pressure. The central concept is that people are often able to compensate for handicaps acquired in early life until ageing reveals their disability. Children who become paralysed from poliomyelitis often make a full recovery and return to normal activity. In later life, however, when muscle and nerve cells are lost through ageing, the damage sustained in childhood may be unmasked and a life becomes blighted by weakness and exhaustion.

In the Helsinki study we found that more of the men and women whose birthweights were in the lower part of the range were receiving treatment for high blood pressure, as we had come to expect. Before the Second World War the Finnish economy was depressed. The fathers of many of the people in the study worked as labourers and lived in poor conditions in small over-crowded houses. Among the children who grew up in these houses low birthweight greatly increased the risks of hypertension, but among the more fortunate, born into the homes of well-paid officials, low birthweight did not increase the risk at all. We do not yet know why this should be, though possible explanations abound, but it reaffirms the point that the biological influences which result in low birthweight have serious consequences in people whose lives follow one path and lesser consequences in those who follow other paths. The pathways are marked out not only by living conditions but by rates of weight gain. Among the labourers' children those who had low birthweight but did not gain weight rapidly in childhood were at less risk than those who had both low birthweight and rapid weight gain. Some paths of growth carry people safely through adversity; others make them vulnerable. Resilience and vulnerability to psychosocial stress are discussed later in this chapter.

DIABETES

Insulin regulates the baby's growth. After birth it is relegated to a lesser, though important role, as housekeeper for the body's sugar, removing sugar from the blood and putting it into the tissues, muscle in particular, where it is used as a source of energy. It is in principle unsurprising that foetal responses to meet the problems of growth in early life translate into problems with the control of sugar in later life.

People develop the common form of diabetes, so-called type 2 diabetes, for two reasons: either they do not respond to the insulin they produce, or they do not make enough of it. Insulin is made by the pancreas in cells called beta cells. The beta cells are largely complete before birth, though development continues during the first five months of infancy. Studies in animals have shown that if the mother is undernourished, her offspring's beta cells are impaired for life. Like the kidney with fewer nephrons, the pancreas of the undernourished foetus has a lifelong reduction in its functional capacity. It is less able to make insulin and meet the challenges of managing the body's sugar. One of these challenges is obesity, which makes the body less responsive, or 'resistant', to insulin, so that more of it has to be made than would otherwise be needed to move glucose out of the blood into the tissues. Reduced ability to make insulin, combined with excess requirement for it, leads eventually to inability to maintain the amount of sugar in the blood at normal levels. Diabetes develops.

Obesity is not the only cause of resistance to insulin. The degree of resistance varies widely between one person and another. Chapter 2 described how 'receptors' in cells establish how sensitive a particular tissue is to hormones that command it – how much hormone is needed before the tissue responds. This sensitivity is set during development. Indian people are exceptionally insensitive, or 'resistant' to insulin. This has led to the familiar conclusion that 'it must be genetic'. However, at any level of body weight children and adults who were small at birth are more resistant than those who were large. This has been shown in many countries – in Europe, the USA, India and China. It seems to be the thin, low-birthweight baby that is most prone to becoming insulin-resistant. Like thin children, thin babies lack muscle though they may also lack fat. Run your fingers down the thigh of a thin newborn baby and you will readily feel the bone because the muscle is sparse. Muscle is the principal tissue on which insulin acts to remove sugar from the blood. It has a low priority for growth in the womb and is readily sacrificed if a baby is undernourished. If muscle does not develop at this time, not only is this a lifelong deficit that leads a person to be less strong and more readily fatigued, but he or she will also be resistant to insulin. The development of insulin resistance in response to undernutrition in the womb could be the result of either constraint or adaptation, as was discussed in Chapter 3. It could be a consequence of the low priority accorded to muscle growth; which is therefore readily sacrificed if resources become scarce. Or it could be adaptive. If the muscles of an undernourished baby become resistant to insulin, more sugar will remain in the blood. This sugar will be available to the brain whose growth is thereby protected. Insulin resistance could be part of a system that develops in the baby to use sugar in a thrifty way. Priority is given to maintaining adequate sugar levels in the blood and it becomes difficult to store it in the body's larder, the muscles. The larder doors are difficult to open. Thrifty handling of sugar becomes 'hard-wired', incorporated into the body's structures and persists through life. But it becomes a liability when food becomes more freely available after birth. The blood becomes flooded with sugar, obesity increases insulin resistance and the larder door becomes more firmly shut.

Although resistance to insulin may be a response to, using Darwin's phrase, the 'conditions of life', genes will, of course, underlie the ability to mount this response. Some babies will do it more readily than others. What a baby's genes do depends on the environment within the womb for which birthweight serves as a marker. It is to be expected, therefore, that the effects of genes in men and women will be conditioned by their birthweight. A given gene may do one thing in people who were small at birth and another in people who were large. The effects of the gene will 'interact' with the effects of birthweight.

Though making predictions is part of the scientific process, one does not necessarily expect one's predictions to be right and neither, if they are correct, does one expect them to be easily demonstrated. Almost as soon as we began to look for 'interactions' between genes and birthweight we found them. One form of a common gene, whose extraordinarily long name is shortened to PPAR gamma, has been shown to promote insulin resistance. From one study to another, however, the findings are inconsistent – a theme that is becoming familiar in this book. If it is inconsistent, the statisticians maintain, truth can only be established by larger studies, not of thousands of people but of tens of thousands, or even hundreds of thousands. Not so, argue the biologists; if it is inconsistent there must be heterogeneity – in some people, one thing happens, in others another. And it proved to be so. In a group of 500 elderly people in Helsinki we found that the effect of this form, or 'polymorphism' of the gene on insulin resistance only occurred in those whose birthweight had been below around 7 pounds (3.2 kg). In people with birthweights higher than this the polymorphism had no effect. To know what the gene was doing in these elderly people it was necessary to know their birthweight, the conditions of life in the womb. And to know what the conditions they had experienced in the womb were doing to them it was necessary to know about their genes. Exactly what one would have predicted, but we were amazed to see it, nonetheless. Since then other genes have been found to interact with birth size and a new chapter of research into life in the womb has begun.

CHOLESTEROL

Cholesterol is an essential component of the 'walls' which enclose cells. It is also required to manufacture hormones. It is made in the liver and circulates in the blood to reach the tissues. The amount of cholesterol in the tissues is maintained at a constant level by a balance between production and excretion, both carried out by the liver. Chapter 1 described how the blood cholesterol levels of middle-aged men and women in Sheffield were found to be predicted by the girth of their abdomen when they were born. Less girth, which indicates less liver, leads to a higher cholesterol level. Poor liver growth in the womb is therefore linked to the maintenance of higher levels of cholesterol in the tissues in later life, whether by greater production or reduced excretion is not known. In animals it is easy to change the activities of the liver permanently by altering the mother's diet in pregnancy. This happens because undernutrition changes the balance of the liver's specialist cells. For example, it increases the number of cells that work to store sugar in the body and reduces the number that break sugars down. Like other organs the liver is plastic and in the womb it is learning the level of activity that is required of it.

After birth the baby receives large amounts of cholesterol from breast milk. There has been considerable speculation that the amount of cholesterol and saturated fat in the mother's milk establishes the way the body handles fat thereafter. We return to this in Chapter 9. The liver remains plastic until around four years of age and, unlike the brain, which grows at its own speed, its growth follows that of the body as a whole. In Hertfordshire the babies who put on weight slowly during infancy had altered levels of cholesterol and other lipids in their blood – presumably because their livers did not grow as well as they might have and structures within the liver were permanently changed.

STRESS

In the womb and during infancy, insulin commands growth: cortisol, the stress hormone, commands differentiation – it enters cells and turns on their specialised functions. It controls the maturation of the lungs and other systems that enable the baby to live independently of the mother after birth. There is a surge of cortisol in the baby as the time of birth approaches. When a baby is undernourished it is stressed; it can increase its production of cortisol, mature rapidly and leave the womb prematurely. Like the tadpole in the drying pond, it can hasten its development and depart for life on land.

After birth, differentiation is mostly complete. Cortisol remains part of the body's responses to stress, but these responses are less exalted than the differentiation they commanded before birth. They prepare the body for 'fight or flight'. Many animals use cortisol to adjust their internal environments to stresses in the external environment. In the breeding season the male Antechinus, a mouse-like animal in which the females have a pouch like kangaroos, increases its cortisol production so that it can withstand the stress of repeated intensive mating. After mating, it dies: a victim of its own cortisol. The amount of cortisol people make when they are stressed, and the sensitivity of their tissues to it, varies widely from one person to another. Could this be linked to their pattern of cortisol production in the womb? There are indications that this is so, that people who were small at birth have more cortisol circulating in their blood and have a heightened cortisol response to stress for the rest of their lives. In the short term this may be unimportant because the excess cortisol does not reach the levels which kill the male Antechinus. But in the long term it could be harmful. When cortisol is used as medication over many months it raises blood pressure and produces insulin resistance. It has been suggested that smaller amounts, produced by the body over many years, have a similar effect.

One of the best-known studies of the occurrence of heart disease is the study of civil servants in Whitehall, the seat of government in Britain. It is the British equivalent of the Framingham study, and why we chose to study such a particular group of people rather than people in a small town is a piece of history in which opportunism and the availability of money played a large part. Senior civil servants enjoy less heart disease and live longer lives than their juniors. Indeed, they are practically immortal, though this is not the result of abstention from the pleasures of life. Their juniors perceive themselves to be more stressed, less in control than their bosses. Could their worse health lie in their inner environments, their different origins from those of the mandarins who control our nation, their greater vulnerability to stress? Did they grow differently in the womb?

For many years a link between heart disease and stress was rejected. Heart disease is a recent disease that accompanies prosperity. Surely it could not be more stressful to be a junior civil servant in London than a millhand in a Lancashire cotton mill one hundred years ago, or a peasant in feudal England, or a sailor at the battle of Trafalgar? We may have overlooked that people can respond violently to the perception of stress or its symbols. The swastika is a universal symbol. To Hindus and Buddhists it is a symbol of peace. To people who experienced the Nazis it is stressful. It may not be the absolute level of life-threatening stress that is important in heart disease, but the response of the internal environment to what is perceived to be stressful. The Whitehall researchers proposed that being at the lower end of a hierarchy, whether at work or socially, was stressful, and evidence to support this is appearing.

The size at birth of the Whitehall civil servants is not known. But answers to questions posed by the Whitehall study are being found in Helsinki. Men in the Helsinki study who have low taxable incomes have more heart disease. Since by world standards they are all relatively affluent, this could reflect a low position in the social hierarchy. It is, however, only men who were small and thin at birth in whom low incomes had this effect. For men who were not thin at birth low incomes, and whatever aspects of social stress or living conditions are related to low income, are without effect on heart disease. They are resilient. The group of men who are most vulnerable to poor living conditions are those who were both small at birth and had rapid weight gain thereafter. This is further evidence that the red areas on our map of England and Wales define a vulnerability to influences acting in later life – vulnerability that originates in the womb.

MOULDING THE INTERNAL ENVIRONMENT

These examples lead to a general conclusion, though it is a tentative one, that calls for more research. The internal environment of each individual is established in the womb and during early childhood. Though it is based on a genetic blueprint, it is moulded by the challenges of development. Among these challenges are matching the rate of growth to the availability of food and, when food is scarce, or the delivery mechanism faulty, as it often is, protecting the growth of key organs, trading off the growth of other organs or speeding up the rate of development. Overcoming these challenges permanently alters the body which, through various processes, becomes more vulnerable to disease in later life. Reduced reserve capacity in organs such as the kidney becomes critical as ageing further reduces the reserve. An internal environment that uses food thriftily is harmful when food becomes abundant. Hormonal settings that are evoked by the stress of undernutrition heighten the body's responses to stress in later life.

When I walk round the medical wards of our hospital, or see patients in the clinic, I see people who mounted successful responses to the challenges of development – responses that enabled them to survive but for which they are now paying the deferred costs.

5

A Forecast from Mother

A SUCCESSFUL PREGNANCY

In a group of babies the risk of heart disease and diabetes falls progressively between the smallest and the largest, up to somewhere around 10 pounds (4.5 kg). Large size at birth, however, is not always beneficial. Among heavy Western babies there are those who are heavy because they are long and muscular: these are at low risk of later disease. However, there are others who are heavy because they are fat rather than because they are muscular. These babies are at increased risk of diabetes and their mothers may themselves develop diabetes in later life.

Because a newborn baby weighs only 6 pounds (2.7 kg), even though born after a full-length pregnancy, it does not denote that he or she is necessarily at increased risk of disease. As described in the last chapter, the risk will be influenced by what has gone before – the genes inherited at conception – and by what follows – childhood growth and living conditions. Babies of a given weight also vary widely in the composition of their bodies. Some are disproportionate, being thin or short, others are proportionate. Each has a different destiny because they are the result of different paths of growth in the womb. After birth some small babies continue to be small, even though they are offered unlimited food. All that excess food achieves is to make them fat, rather than taller and more muscular. It is as though their path of growth before birth is one into which they have settled. Other small babies, if given sufficient food, will have rapid 'catch up' in weight and height, as though their slow growth before birth conflicted with an aspiration for more rapid growth. Catching up during infancy is beneficial. Large babies are less likely to become ill with infections. After one year, however,

78

continued rapid gain in weight becomes harmful and increases the risk of later disease. Why this should be so is discussed further in Chapter 8.

Small infants, like small children, differ one from another. Some small infants were small at every stage of life. They are, as it were, miniatures. Others, including millions born in developing countries, become small because of the conditions to which they are exposed around the time of weaning. Because different parts of the body grow most rapidly at different times, the body proportions of undernourished infants will be affected. Their legs, which grow rapidly in early childhood, will be short in relation to the length of their backs, which grow rapidly in the womb.

People sometimes come up to me after lectures and say, 'I only weighed 5 pounds when I was born, but I was a twin: do I have a problem?' To which the answer is, 'Not necessarily.' A baby that weighs 5 pounds because it had to share the womb with another human being is biologically different from a single-born baby of the same weight. Competing for food in the womb induces a variety of responses that become 'hard-wired' in twins. They are different. Some twins seem to settle for less at an early stage of the pregnancy and grow slowly. Others grow more rapidly, but in late pregnancy when the babies are large and competition for food severe, they are unable to sustain their growth. It seems likely that these will be the twins at risk of later disease, but as yet we do not know.

The geneticists who assert that events at conception are more important than subsequent events in determining heart disease and diabetes, an assertion that is simplistic and denies developmental plasticity, point to the similar experiences of these diseases among identical twins. If one develops a disease the other is likely to. The similarity is closer than that between non-identical twins. Geneticists sometimes forget that identical twins, coming from the same fertilised egg, share a placenta, while non-identical twins do not: each of the twin eggs implants separately. As a result, identical twins' similar experience of disease could reflect their shared food supply more than their identical genes.

One reason we have remained largely ignorant about mothers' diets in pregnancy is that we have set modest targets for babies which contrast with our aspirations for our children after birth. A century ago people were grateful if a child survived and grew to a reasonable size. Today we take this for granted. We concern ourselves with their physical abilities, their behaviour, their emotional and intellectual development. But for babies we still require only survival and a reasonable body weight.

A quarter of all baby boys born in Britain today are thin, many others are short, though of around average birthweight. Our acceptance of this echoes our acceptance of thin and stunted children a century ago. In the early twentieth century 'hereditarians', of whom there were many on both sides of the Atlantic, justified the continuing presence of the thin, stunted children of the poor by saying they were 'inferior stock' doomed from the moment of conception, unalterably handicapped. Eventually we realised that the puny children, in the slums of cities and the fields of poor farms, were not part of the natural order of things. Motivated partly by the need for armies of tall, strong young men, Europeans took steps to improve the nutrition and living conditions of their children. With one striking exception, France, babies in the womb were largely neglected.

The new target for pregnancy cannot now be simply a reasonably sized baby that is not deformed. It is a baby whose structures and metabolic behaviour will optimise its health in the particular circumstances into which it is born.

THE MOTHER CONTROLS GROWTH

A baby's growth is influenced by its genes. When short, slim young women from Thailand marry tall European men, the baby may need to be delivered by Caesarean section because it is too large to be delivered through the birth canal. It is, however, the delivery of food and oxygen to the baby that governs the baby's growth and its size at birth. As the nutritionist Ronald McCance wrote long ago, 'The size attained *in utero* depends on the services which the mother is able to supply. These are mainly food and accommodation.'

The mother exerts a stronger effect on the growth of the baby than the father. The birthweights of babies from the same mother, but by different fathers, tend to be similar. The birthweights of babies with the same father but from different mothers are different. A striking illustration of the dominance of the environment in the womb on the growth of babies comes from the experience of women who become pregnant with an egg donated by another woman. The egg is taken from the donor, fertilised in the laboratory and placed in the womb of the recipient. The birthweights of babies born after ovum donation are strongly related to the weights of the recipient mothers, but are unrelated to the weights of the women who donated the eggs.

THE PADDED CELL

Because babies seemed able to grow to reasonable size, almost irrespective of what the mothers eat in late pregnancy, the view has developed that the baby in the womb is a highly successful parasite, like a tick or a leech, able to take from the mother whatever it requires and satisfy its modest needs. For so long as the baby is in the womb it seems able to fend for itself. Not until late pregnancy, when it grows rapidly, do its food requirements become substantial, and even these, it seems, are readily satisfied at the mother's expense. In the wartime famine in Holland, pregnant women lost weight but their babies continued to grow. In the developed world most babies achieve a birthweight within the normal range. Thus in the womb the baby seems protected, buffered from the world by the mother's body, a shield pierced only by poisons or dangerous infections. Alone in its padded cell, it lives out its genetic potential to emerge preordained and bespoke to greetings of, 'It's got father's chin, mother's eyes.'

Such a comfortable picture is far from the true one. It resonates with the position on child growth adopted by the hereditarians a century ago. Other than dwarfs, the weights of almost all children were somewhere within a normal range (the word 'normal' means 'usual' not 'optimal'). The children of the poor were stunted and thin because they came from genetically inferior stock. There was no compelling reason to change things. Around the world the babies of the poor are stunted and thin, though even in India many babies achieve 6 or 7 pounds.

The womb is not a padded cell. The baby is sensitive to what happens outside its warm pool. Every pulse of its mother brings it a various and varying supply of foods. These shape its structures and mould its systems. They, the ingredients, combine with the genetic recipe to create a unique human being. Walk around a nursery; look at the newborn babies. See the fat one, the thin one, the one with the large head. Were these specified at conception? Are the babies of poorer people thin and short because it was so ordained? Or is it the food they never had?

THE BABY'S SOURCE OF FOOD

For two hundred years interest in mothers' diets was focused on the special dietary requirements of later pregnancy, judged against the birthweight of the baby. Numerous studies examined whether the quality of the diet eaten by a pregnant woman influenced the birthweight of the baby. The results were various and contradictory. Even the expected relationship between total food intake and birthweight was less than had been expected – just a few hundred grams.

After the Allied armies failed to establish a bridgehead at Arnhem in the autumn of 1944, the occupying forces made reprisals against the population of western Holland. Tight restrictions on food supplies were imposed and official rations were at starvation levels. Old people died, babies were stillborn, many women ceased to menstruate, yet the birthweights of babies who were already in the womb when the Dutch famine began fell, on average, by only ¾ pound (0.3 kg). Even the prolonged and exceptionally severe famine during the siege of Leningrad led to only a 1¼ pound (0.6 kg) fall in the average birthweight. Despite the conditions the babies were able to grow but, we now know, at a heavy price. Today, fifty odd years later, those Dutch babies have more diabetes. To achieve growth they used food in a thrifty way. As has already been described, they became insulin-resistant. This proved a handicap when starvation was followed by affluence.

The baby does not depend only on what the mother eats each day. That would be too dangerous a strategy. It utilises the mother's food reserves, some of which are in stores while others are incorporated in the mother's muscle and fat from which they are liberated by daily protein and fatty acids 'turnover'. Although muscle cells cannot divide, they are continuously reconstructed. Each day a young man breaks down and renews 3 per cent of his muscle. The proteins within the cells are broken down, released into the blood and re-formed. This phenomenon, called 'turnover', occurs in other organs and tissues, including the brain and fat. Bone continuously turns over, forming and resorbing, taking in calcium and releasing it into the blood. Though the exterior of the adult body may be constant, within it is like a beehive in a dynamic state of breakdown and renewal. This dynamic state confers flexibility and allows the body to adapt to a changing external environment, different foods, varied activities. For the baby it is an important source of food, as the mother is constantly enriching the nutrients in her blood from her own body.

DOWN THE GENERATIONS

Studies in domestic animals demonstrate how birth size is controlled by the mother rather than the genetic inheritance from both parents, though this contributes. In a famous experiment, small Shetland ponies were crossed with large shire-horses. The foals were smaller at birth when the Shetland pony was the mother than when the shire-horse was the mother. As the genetic composition of the two crosses was similar, this implied that the Shetland mother had constrained the growth of the foetus. There were similar results when South Devon cattle, the largest breed of cattle in the British Isles, were crossed with Dexter cattle, the smallest breed. The results of these cross-breeding experiments

THE BEST START IN LIFE

are supported by experiments in which animal embryos are removed from the mothers' wombs and placed in another mother. Size at birth is determined by the size of the womb into which the embryo is transferred.

Human mothers who have babies that are termed 'growth-retarded' – who weigh less than 5½ pounds (2.5 kg) despite being born at around the expected date – tend to have had low birth-weight themselves. Women who were small at birth are at twice the risk of having a small baby. This suggests that, like Shetland ponies, mothers constrain the growth of their babies, but the degree of constraint they exert was established when they themselves were in the womb. Sisters tend to have babies with similar birthweights because, having experienced a common level of constraint when they were in the womb, they exert a similar level of constraint on their own babies. This constraint is thought to principally reflect the mother's limited capacity to transfer nutrients to her baby, her ability to supply food rather than provide accommodation. We do not understand the processes by which slow growth of a baby girl in the womb impairs her later ability to nourish her own babies. One possibility is that at birth small girls have fewer blood vessels going to the womb, part of a more general poverty of blood vessels in small babies, and this may be a lifelong deficit which reduces the supply of food to the next generation in the womb.

The human baby responds to its mother's mother. The egg from which your life began was formed when your mother was a baby. She was born with all the eggs she would ever have. Their number, and perhaps quality, were influenced by your grand-mother's womb. Sensitivity of the baby's organs and systems to more than one generation allows it to adapt to the level of nutrition which has prevailed over many years rather than only to that at the time of its conception. The human mother is predicting for her baby the likely availability of food after birth through information acquired over several generations. In our evolutionary past, when periodic famines occurred through crop failures, wars and pestilence, this ability to inform the baby about long-term trends in food availability may have been important. The pathways to disease today began long ago.

Experiments in animals have demonstrated that the diet of a given generation may affect the offspring for several generations. A colony of rats was given a diet deficient in protein. When the colony was refed with a normal diet it took three generations before foetal growth and development were restored to normal. If pregnant rats exercise excessively, foetal growth is reduced for two generations. It follows that as women in places such as India and China cease to be chronically malnourished, or carry out heavy manual labour throughout pregnancy, it will take more than one generation before the full benefits reach the baby. India underwent the 'Green Revolution' during 1967 to 1978. Expansion of farmland and improvements in farming practices increased the availability of food and abolished large-scale famine. Nevertheless, the average birthweight in India remains around 6 pounds (2.7 kg). Similarly, for people who emigrate to western countries from poorly nourished communities, Indian migrants to Europe, Mexican migrants to the USA, more than one generation will be required before the growth of their babies increases to the level of the host country.

THE SENSITIVE EMBRYO

Because the embryo and foetus are small in early pregnancy, it used to be assumed that undernutrition could not be a problem. We now know, however, that this is not the case. When, for example, pigs are given food that is low in protein from the time of mating, the piglets are already small in mid-pregnancy – though some are smaller than others as competition for food between brother and sister begins early. This shows that undernutrition slows growth through processes other than the simple lack of building blocks with which to make tissues: it gives signals which command slow growth. It is becoming increasingly clear that nutrition affects those of the baby's hormones that control its growth and the most important of these is insulin. Studies of animals show that when a mother reduces her food intake, the baby reduces the amount of insulin it makes and this slows its growth. This may be a direct effect of the reduced amount of protein and sugar in the mother's blood, or it may depend on the mother's own hormones, whose production varies with her nutritional state. Either way, insulin and hormones similar to it (the so-called insulin-like growth factors) give the baby the ability to match the rate at which it grows to the availability of food. When food is scarce the baby is able to slow its growth in a coordinated way and does not have to wait until the building blocks are exhausted. Such an eventuality would selectively and unpredictably damage particular organs.

Through effects of food or hormones in the mother's blood, the embryo and foetus seem to be sensitive to the mother's nutritional state from a very early stage of pregnancy. Studies in animals show that even before the embryo invades the wall of the womb (on the eighth day after fertilisation in humans) it is sensitive to the mother. There seems no reason why this sensitivity should begin at fertilisation: while the egg matures in the first two weeks of the menstrual cycle it could be changed by the nutrients that reach it. This line of thought leads on to ideas which, until recently, were seldom articulated. Since a girl is born with all the eggs she will ever release, will the quality of the eggs be reduced if she is undernourished? We do not know. But alterations in the quality of an egg could potentially alter every cell in the body of the baby that egg may one day become.

Insights into the effects of nutrition on the early embryo have come from 'test tube' techniques in which eggs are removed from the mother and allowed to mature and become fertilised outside her body before being returned. These techniques are widely used in domestic animals. The composition of the fluid in which the eggs are kept can change the foetus's rate of growth. In farm animals, this leaves a legacy of developmental changes that alter their size and health at birth, their growth after birth and their reproductive performance. We know little about this in humans, but human reproduction cannot be divorced from that of other animals.

One demonstration of the astonishing downstream consequences of early nutrition comes from the birth of giant farm animals. When test tube techniques were introduced into animal breeding, lambs of twice the normal size began to appear. Large calves were born with enlarged hearts that remained large for the rest of their lives. Since, in humans, an enlarged heart increases the risk of a heart attack, and since among Dutch people exposed to famine it was those conceived during the famine who developed the highest rates of heart disease, it is impossible to resist the speculation that heart attacks may originate at the earliest stage in life.

This remains a speculation. In principle, however, it would be unsurprising if nutrition of an early embryo had profound long-term effects. While a living thing consists of only a few cells, there is the possibility of altering the entire body into which it will grow. Later on it is only the body parts that are at 'sensitive periods' of development at the time which can readily be changed. At present little is known about which nutrients and hormones the embryo is sensitive to. But though its demands are minute, the embryo's need for nutrients is particular. Relatively minor changes can lead to major alterations in its subsequent growth and development. We do not know if there are times before or after fertilisation when the egg and early embryo are especially sensitive. In farm animals the female's nutrition influences the egg while it matures, before ovulation, possibly through the effects of nutrition on her hormone levels. Whether this is so in women is not known.

Recent studies in mice show that the mother's nutrition at the time of conception not only affects the growth of her embryos but may reset their blood pressures for life. When the protein in the diet of female mice was reduced for a brief two-day period around the time of mating, the structure of the embryos was visibly changed at a stage of development when they were no more than hollow balls of cells. At birth they were smaller and had smaller livers. After birth they gained weight rapidly and developed raised blood pressure. The brief exposure to a low-protein diet did not affect litter size or lead to miscarriages, but its profound effects on body size illustrate the extreme sensitivity of growth of the early embryo to the environment afforded by the mother.

We do not know what in the mother the human embryo

senses, but 12,000 young women in Southampton have agreed to help us find out. They come from a wide variety of social backgrounds and their diets, body size, living conditions and lifestyles vary across the whole range seen in Britain today. At the outset of the study they were not pregnant. Each of them was visited at home by one of our nurses who recorded their diets, measured their body size and shape, and asked them about their health. A blood sample was taken and when, in due course, some became pregnant they told us as soon as they knew. Their baby's growth was measured by ultrasound scans in early, mid and late pregnancy. For the first time it will be possible to link a mother's body size and shape, diet and hormone levels to her baby's growth in early pregnancy.

TESTING THE WIND

The idea that children are plastic as they develop is familiar. We know that the way we bring up our children alters their characters, skills, attitudes, moods, for life. 'The child is father to the man,' wrote Wordsworth. 'Give me a child until he is seven years old and I will give you the man,' declared the Jesuits. The brain is incomplete at birth. Though the cells are in place they have not been connected. The connections are not closely specified by genes. Michael was not born to be intelligent, manly, withdrawn; he became so largely through experience. Parents accept the responsibility of controlling the forum in which the mind develops. We accept the chance of either happy, fulfilled children or children whose minds are flawed. We accept that we will never know why one child is less fulfilled than its brothers or sisters. Was it biological destiny? Was it something we did? Plasticity does not begin in infancy and early childhood. It ends there. By the time of birth most of the organs and systems are complete. Only a few, including the brain, the liver and immune system, remain open to experience, requiring stimulation from the world beyond the womb to fashion their final form.

The conclusion that the baby is a highly successful parasite, able to satisfy its small demands whatever the state of the mother, came from the observation that babies seemed able to grow to a reasonable size almost irrespective of what the mother ate in late pregnancy. There is, however, another possible conclusion. Babies, like children, are good at growing, however bad the conditions, though growth may have high costs. Through wars and famines children keep on growing. They do not grow as tall as they otherwise would have grown, but the deficit is modest, an inch or so. Babies too can adjust and grow, but much of their body is plastic and their adjustments tend to become a permanent part of them. A heart attack, a stroke, diabetes, seem to be deferred costs of successful adaptations which allowed the baby to survive and grow.

Like infants, babies adjust their growth rates to the amount of food they receive from their mothers. In doing so they adapt to the world into which they will be born. A large baby born among chronically undernourished people is more likely to die than a small baby because its needs are greater. The forecast which the mother gives her baby does not only affect its body size. A baby in an undernourished mother will alter the way in which it handles sugar. It will become thrifty, maintaining high levels of sugar in its bloodstream for the benefit of the brain and other organs, rather than storing it in its muscle. Once adopted, this thrifty behaviour becomes its way of life. To be thrifty is neither good nor bad. It is appropriate to scarcity. But when, after birth, scarcity is replaced by abundance it is inappropriate.

MANIPULATING THE BABY'S FOOD

This book is written in the comfort of southern England. Food is plentiful, sufficient for each mother and baby. A mother should not have to sacrifice her own needs to those of her children. All mothers should be able to offer their babies the best possible array of nutrients in the knowledge that they are being born into plenty and this is likely to be their lot through their lives. This is not so throughout the world.

Much is known about the effects of scarcity in the womb followed by abundance after birth. Many immigrants who come into the USA and Europe from poorer countries have followed this path. Mexican immigrants in the USA and immigrants from India in Europe have exceptionally high rates of diabetes. Hereditarians attribute this to unknown genes acquired through natural selection in impoverished places. Mexican and Indian people, they are suggesting, are from 'inferior stock', unable to adapt to better diets, destined to thrive only in want. The thesis of this book is that these high rates of diabetes are due more to the changing conditions within the lifetime of an individual than to the natural selection of genes.

Less is known about lifetime journeys in which abundance in the womb is followed by scarcity after birth. This needs to be studied. If a pregnant woman boosts her diet with high intakes of supplements the baby could adopt a profligate way of handling some nutrients, become a 'profligate phenotype' rather than a 'thrifty phenotype'. A person with a profligate metabolism will be more vulnerable to shortage; will become deficient at levels of food consumption that are adequate for people who are thrifty. Pathways to health may require that whatever the baby gets, the child and adult should get. Little is known about this in humans.

A journey from excess to shortage is not uncommon in animals, many of whom live on food that goes through cycles of abundance and scarcity. A digression to the Arctic reveals how, in times of plenty, the vixen anticipates future scarcity and reduces the number of young she will carry in the womb. The owl, meanwhile, reduces the food it carries to its nestlings and keeps more for itself. Food shortage increases the numbers of miscarriages and deaths among the young. This happened in the Dutch famine. Parental strategies to deal with periodic famine may include both minimisation of deaths and maximisation of the fitness of the survivors. The red fox, *Vulpes vulpes*, lives in Arctic Sweden and feeds on voles, whose numbers fluctuate through the seasons and over three- to four-year cycles. The vixens mate in January or February and when the spring comes in May they are already in late pregnancy or lactating. This doubles their food requirements and the food supply becomes critical. Matters are so arranged, however, that the number of cubs they carry is appropriate to the abundance of voles in the area: the more abundant the voles, the more cubs are born. How is such a useful adaptation achieved?

The number of cubs is determined by the number of eggs released from the vixens' ovaries before mating. In mammals, food shortage reduces the number of eggs that are released, because it reduces the amount of a hormone, gonadotrophin, which is made in the pituitary gland and stimulates the ripening of follicles in the ovary. Because of the seasonal cycles the abundance of voles in the mating season, January to February, is not, however, closely related to the abundance in the spring when the cubs are born. Somehow when they mate the vixens respond, not to the amount of food they are eating at the time, but to the amount they predict will be available in the spring. It is in the interests of both the mother and her cubs that she does not carry more cubs than she can nourish during late pregnancy and after birth, when voles are still scarce but the mother's requirements are large. How, in January, does she predict the number of voles that will be around in May?

It might, of course, be inherited knowledge, like the salmon's knowledge of the routes and timetables of its wanderings through the oceans. But fluctuations in vole numbers vary from year to year, and between one locality and the next. A plastic system operated by an environmental cue seems a better option. But what could the cue be? It is, it seems, the hormone levels in the vole. During the winter voles only breed if their numbers are increasing – when an upward fluctuation in the cycle is in process. When they are breeding they will produce more gonadotrophin hormone. This will be ingested by the vixens that eat them, and will stimulate them to produce more eggs.

Another Arctic creature that preys on voles, the Tengmalm's owl, exhibits another form of anticipatory behaviour. During the increase phase of a vole cycle, female owls produce the largest clutches of eggs and, through the night, males fly back and forth feeding the females and their offspring. When the vole cycle is at its peak, however, and food is at its most abundant, the males lose interest and deliver less food to the nest. After midnight they spend more time feeding themselves and resting. When they return to the nest they are less interested in defending it from pine martins who come to take the eggs. Is this because, after the peak, vole numbers may crash abruptly? Many offspring will die and it may be advantageous for the parents to provide a few well-fed owlets rather than many starving ones.

The red fox and Tengmalm's owl anticipate future food supply. They change the allocation of food (voles) to their offspring by reducing the number of babies and changing their feeding behaviour. The human mother only carries one baby and has fewer options. The reduction in fertility and higher rate of miscarriages and stillbirths in the Dutch famine could be viewed as adaptive, reducing the demand on the mothers.

The human baby develops through biological processes we share with other animals, processes that were created through evolution and are a centrepiece of evolutionary strategy. Processes over which, before birth, the mother exerts no control, though her body provides the arena. After birth she, like the male Tengmalm's owl, negotiates with her offspring. The negotiations determine the length of breastfeeding, the age at weaning and may involve conflict.

CONFLICT BETWEEN MOTHERS AND BABIES

The limited amount of food that is available to many mothers around the world heightens conflict of interests between mother and baby. Elephant seals come ashore to breed on the island of South Georgia. Once on the beach, the mothers do not eat. They nourish their pups solely from the reserves of fat and protein stored in their bodies. The proportion of the food reserves made available to the pups may be critical to both mother and child. Mothers that expend a large proportion of their reserves on their pups may compromise their own survival to the next breeding season or reduce the number of offspring they have in the future. On the other hand, if their pups are born small and thin, their chances of surviving to breeding age are reduced. The size of a pup is a compromise between the future reproductive success of the mother and the survival of the pup. Male pups are heavier at birth than females and the smallest elephant seal mothers only give birth to females, which suggests that they abort male pups. This may be an advantage if they are unable to raise a male pup to a viable size without jeopardising their own survival.

The theory of 'parent-child conflict' proposes that natural selection encourages babies to demand more resources from parents than parents are selected to give. Three sets of genes have different interests: the mother's genes, the baby's genes derived from the mother and the baby's genes derived from the father. If the genes of any individual baby are permitted to make excessive demands on the mother, it will, like the male pup in the young elephant seal, prejudice her ability to pass her genes on to future children. During evolution a baby's genes will have been selected to increase the transfer of food to it, from the mother, so that it can grow larger. Big babies are more likely to survive than small babies. A mother's genes will have been selected to limit transfer of food to the baby in order to protect the mother, and to ensure her survival and that of her other children, born and unborn. What is best for a baby need not be best for its mother, or so it seems.

The genes that the baby has derived from the father, however, have been selected to take more resources from the mother's tissues than the genes derived from the mother. The father's genes promote the baby's growth irrespective of the mother's well-being, for he can have more children by other mothers. The conflict between maternal and paternal genes over the nutritional demands that the foetus imposes on its mother may explain why genes derived from one parent can 'imprint', or override, the expression of those derived from the other. An intriguing, though speculative, theory suggests that toxaemia and other diseases of pregnancy originate in the turmoil of this genetic conflict.

Beyond these fascinating genetic theories it is clear that in the distribution of food there is often conflict between parents and children. In times of famine Chinese peasants gave their children away. When adolescent girls become pregnant there is conflict between their need for food in order to continue to grow and the needs of their baby. The blue petrel alternates long feeding trips out to sea with short feeding trips near the shore. Although the short trips increase the rate at which the chicks are fed, the father and mother lose weight. On long trips they feed themselves and restore their weight while the chicks have to wait four times longer for food. A human mother may wish to breastfeed her baby for six months, but may be unable to do so if she is working away from home, and the income and well-being of herself and her family requires that this continues. This is discussed further in Chapter 9. Meanwhile, the next chapter discusses food in pregnancy when, in Western societies at least, there should be sufficient to avoid conflict and satisfy the needs of both mother and baby.

6

Defining a Balanced Diet

A NEW UNDERSTANDING

We have reached a new understanding of the importance of women's diets before and during pregnancy, and of their long-term effects on the health of the baby. In the past we focused our attention on diet in the second half of pregnancy and we studied the effects of single nutrients, such as protein, or folic acid, or zinc, or iron, or magnesium, or calcium on the weight of the baby. Women are advised to take extra folic acid before conceiving. Insofar as this will prevent a rare congenital disorder, spina bifida, this is prudent, but folic acid has many functions as well as its specific ones on the spinal cord. By directing our attention at nutrients rather than foods, we failed to take account of the effects of one nutrient on another. We wrongly assumed that, because birthweight is difficult to manipulate by changing women's diets in late pregnancy, growth does not importantly depend on nutrition. We assumed that, because a baby is small in early pregnancy, and therefore needs only small amounts of food, it obtains everything it needs. We overlooked that food can affect the embryo through the powerful hormonal signals it evokes in the mother. We failed to study the large differences between individual women in the way their bodies handle food and make nutrients available to the baby. We confused the advice given to pregnant women by using pregnancy as an opportunity to give out health messages about the possible effects of fats and sugars on a woman's long-term health.

But there is a way forward. Our knowledge of mothers' diets in places that now have low rates of heart disease points to the success of traditional diets. Modern nutritional science points clearly to the importance of a balanced and varied diet. The knowledge we have acquired from domestic animals shows beyond doubt that the correct feeding of females must begin long before pregnancy.

LESSONS OF HISTORY

History offers some simple and reassuring messages about what women should eat in pregnancy. During the first two decades of the twentieth century life expectation in Britain increased by twelve years, and there were similar trends elsewhere in Europe and the USA. A number of influences contributed to this remarkable extension of the lifespan, including the abolition of famine, improvements in hygiene and sanitation towards the end of the nineteenth century, and advances in medical knowledge. The dominant influence, however, seems to have been the so-called 'escape from hunger'.

It is estimated that towards the end of the eighteenth century the average calorie intake in England was similar to that in India today, while that in France was lower, similar to that in Rwanda today. At such low calorie intakes many people must have starved and the capacity for physical work would be low. Improvements in the supply of food over the next two centuries allowed British, French and other Western populations to become taller and heavier. Chapter 1 briefly described how strong and fit young people from the countryside were drawn into London in the nineteenth century by the prospect of high wages. 'The countrymen drawn in [to London] are mainly the cream of the youth of the villages, travelling not so often vaguely in search of work as definitely to seek a known economic advantage . . .' Booth wrote.

It is the result of the conditions of life in great towns, and especially in this the greatest town of all, that muscular strength and energy get gradually used up; the second generation of Londoners is of lower physique and has less power of persistent work than the first; and the third generation (where it exists) is lower than the second . . .

London is to a great extent nourished by the literal consumption of bone and sinew from the country; by the
absorption every year of large numbers of persons of
stronger physique, who leaven the whole mass, largely
direct the industries, raise the standard of health and
comfort, and keep up the rate of growth of the great city
only to give place in their turn to a fresh set of recruits,
after London life for one or two generations has reduced
them to the level of those among whom they live.

Thus the poor food and poor living conditions in cities and towns
at that time reduced the physique of the men and women who
lived in them. 'Take indifferently twenty well-fed husbandmen
and compare them with twenty industrial workers who have
equal means of support,' wrote Charles Thackrah, founder of
Occupational Medicine, in 1832, 'and the superiority of the
agricultural peasants in health, vigour and size will be obvious.'
Towns were bad for babies as well.

The child of the well-fed, well-worked, cheerful, happy
woman, living in a sunlit airy habitation, is at birth the
finest specimen of its kind. On the other hand what a
miserable sight do the newborn babies of our courts and
alleys, and of the pampered, tight-laced, high-heeled,
lazy, lounging, carriage-possessing women of the higher
classes present! The extremes meet: the poor blanched
creature, half-starved, over-worked, shut up in some close
sunless dwelling, brings forth fruit very like that of her
pale-faced, over-fed, under-worked sofa-loving sister of
the mansion and of the palace . . . Clearly then we may
take it for granted that the development of the fruit within the womb can be modified for good and for ill.

What was it a hundred years ago in the villages of England,
especially those in the south and east of the country, which made
the people healthier and taller? Some of the accommodation in
the villages, the single-roomed cottages and hovels, were as bad as

that in the towns. The people in the villages were poorer than those earning wages in the towns. They were not, however, exposed to the high levels of infectious illness which accompanies the dense inhabitation of towns and stunts the growth of children. And their diets were superior.

In a recent survey of elderly women in six areas of England, a woman who worked in rural Hertfordshire as an upstairs maid in the 1920s described her diet: 'We had four wonderful meals a day . . . An excellent breakfast of porridge, egg dishes or bacon. Lunch was always meat and vegetables and a pudding of sorts. Tea was bread and butter and cake, and supper was usually cold meat, bubble and squeak or a cheese dish.'

The daughter of a labourer growing up in a northern industrial town at the same time recalled, 'I didn't go hungry but we'd no luxuries. Breakfast and tea would be bread and butter mostly. On a Sunday morning we had a bit of cooked bacon, when my dad was working, just a little bit like that and my dad's words were, "Now then, little bits of bacon and big lumps of bread."'

The undernutrition of girls and young women in industrial Britain may have been compounded by preferential feeding of boy children and of men in manual occupations, and by the conditions of their own occupations. In areas where there was little employment for women, notably coal-mining areas, girls were encouraged to marry at a young age and to have large families, which may have further reduced their nutritional state.

In Europe in the past, the frequency of death among newborn babies was a measure of the level of malnutrition in a population. The low death rates among the agricultural communities of southern and eastern England denoted the good nutrition of the mothers. Anecdotally, from the stories of elderly women and writings at the time, it is easy to characterise the good diet which girls and young women enjoyed in childhood, adolescence, before and during pregnancy. The diet was adequate, balanced and varied. People have tried to identify which particular nutrients may have led to the steep fall in deaths of mothers and their babies in the last century. 'Unfit to be a mother through under-

nutrition' was an accepted verdict on a maternal deatl
example of rickets, due to lack of vitamin D, befor€
sought a single culprit. They failed. It is not particular nutric.
but a varied and balanced diet which successfully nourishes a
mother and her baby.

THE FRENCH PARADOX

Heart attacks are uncommon in France, especially in the south.
Sit in a café in Toulouse, watch the cigarette smoke rising from
the nearby tables, read the menu of rich food and wonder why
you are in a place with among the lowest rates of heart attacks in
Europe.

The Nobel Prize winner, Albert Szent-Györgyi, wrote that
'for every complex problem there is a simple, easy to understand,
incorrect answer'. Hitherto, only simple explanations – such as
the protective effects of red wine, garlic or onions – have been
brought forward to explain why French people have low rates of
coronary heart disease despite their 'unhealthy' lifestyles. Not
surprisingly, these simple ideas have not stood the test of time. In
1871 the demoralising defeat in the Franco-Prussian War, together
with concerns about the small number of children in the country,
through a combination of low birth rate and high infant mortality, led to fears that the French army would soon be inadequate
and that France would cease to be a military power. Over the next
thirty years various measures were introduced to protect the
nutrition and health of the country's children. School meals were
established: by 1904, when the *Lancet* sent a representative to
Paris to report on this, a meal (soup, meat and vegetables) was
being provided to every schoolchild. In both Paris and the
provinces there were infant welfare centres promoting breastfeeding and, when this failed, providing sterilised cows' milk
from milk depots. The communes established after the
Revolution provided a framework within which national
directives could be translated into local action. Communes took
responsibility for the welfare of pregnant women.

In Britain the Intergovernmental Committee set up in 1903 revealed that many children were malnourished and deprived, fuelling a series of public health programmes for pregnant women, infants and children. As they devised these welfare programmes, medical officers in Britain looked to 'the French system'. There were other European countries to which they may also have looked. In the seventeenth century Holland became the world's richest nation. Its 2 million inhabitants dominated world trade. Travellers at the time remarked on the surprising variety of the diet of the labouring people: fish, dairy products, fruit and vegetables were widely available. Women held an important place in society and their well-being during pregnancy was a matter of general concern. Today, the Dutch are one of the tallest populations in the world, a testament to generations of good nutrition.

Did better nourishment of girls, better nutrition in pregnancy and better infant feeding protect the generations of French people born from the turn of the century onwards from coronary heart disease? Perhaps the French population successfully 'escaped from hunger' without an epidemic of coronary heart disease by focusing improved nutrition on mothers, babies and young children, by making available to them a diet that was adequate, varied and balanced.

THE IMPORTANCE OF VARIETY

The balanced diet that is a feature of many traditional diets is partly the result of eating a wide variety of foods. Last month I was taken to a restaurant for truck drivers in western Thailand. Our simple meal, at the most modest of costs, contained eighteen different kinds of food: vegetable soup, pork, chicken, fish, shrimp, prawns, rice, potatoes, noodles, beans, chilli, mushrooms, cauliflower, carrots, apple, pineapple, banana and mangoes – certainly a varied and balanced meal! Variety of food is, in part, generated by cultivation and seasonal changes in availability, and in part by a natural desire for palatable food. Variety of foods brings with it a wide range of nutrients, about some of which we still know little. We do know that for the body to use one nutrient others are required, and that tissues are not made of single nutrients; instead, one must be combined with others. In the daily activities of the body, the need for one nutrient is affected by the availability of others. Often there is more than one route by which we solve the challenges of providing energy and maintaining our inner environment. We can, for example, obtain energy from carbohydrate or from protein or from fat or from alcohol. Each brings with it a different requirement for other nutrients.

THE IMPORTANCE OF BALANCE

Forty years ago a new obstetrician was appointed in a Scottish town. He cared deeply about the health of the pregnant women in his care. Many of the families in this steel town were on low wages and the Scottish diet is historically poor. Foods rich in protein were expensive. At that time it was received wisdom that toxaemia, a common illness in pregnancy, which threatens the life of both mother and baby, was the result of lack of protein. The obstetrician therefore encouraged the town's pregnant women to eat a pound of red meat every day. In a booklet given to each expectant mother, he wrote, 'Quantity of meat is more important than quality. As it may be difficult to eat enough meat at meal-times the use of cooked meat, especially corned beef, rather than fruit or biscuits, is advised to assuage hunger between meals.' He discouraged mothers from eating foods that were rich in carbo-hydrate, because excessive weight gain in pregnancy was also thought to be linked to toxaemia. 'Do not eat potatoes or chips, or bread – either white, brown, malted or toasted – rolls, scones, cakes or biscuits of any kind.'

The birthweights of the town's babies fell. Though an unwanted surprise at the time, this has been shown in other studies where the diets of poorer women have been supplemented with protein. When a group of these Scottish babies was exam-ined thirty years later their blood pressures were raised. The more meat the mothers had eaten, the higher the blood pressures of the children, now adults. If mothers had eaten few green vegetables, the blood pressures were even higher. What had gone wrong?

The normal balance of the diets had been perturbed. In the body proteins are broken down into their components, amino acids. These must either be used as building blocks for new tissues or they must be put to other uses or disposed of. To use or dispose of them requires energy, the main sources of which are carbohydrate foods such as bread and potatoes, which the pregnant women were specifically advised to avoid. It also requires other nutrients – folic acid and B vitamins – the natural sources of which include bread and potatoes. The unbalanced diet of the Scottish women not only failed to provide the energy and nutrients needed by the baby, but may also have harmed it in other ways. High-protein diets are now known to stress the body, which responds by making more of the stress hormone, cortisol. There is preliminary evidence that the Scottish babies were stressed by their mothers' diets and that this is still apparent in the way they respond to stress today.

Forty years ago, in another Scottish town, the diets of women – many of whom were similarly poor – were documented. This time no attempt was made to persuade them to change what they ate. Like the other town, the mothers – and there were relatively few – who had high intakes of protein and low intakes of carbohydrate foods had small babies with small placentas. Forty years later these babies had raised blood pressure.

By today's standards, most of the other mothers in the town had low protein intakes. Where these low protein intakes were combined with high intakes of carbohydrate foods, the babies also had small placentas and raised blood pressure forty years later. The adverse effects on the growth of babies of diets low in protein are well known in developing countries, where protein foods tend to be more scarce and expensive than carbohydrate foods. This is because low-protein diets provide too few building blocks and the baby cannot grow properly. We do not know why the combination of this and high energy supplies from carbohydrate is especially damaging, but one way of viewing it is that the availability of energy encourages the baby to grow more rapidly than the supply of building blocks allows. If there are many bricklayers but few bricks, building will rapidly come to a halt. It is clear, therefore, that there is a desirable balance, as either too much or too little protein in relation to carbohydrate has undesirable effects.

If the need for a balanced diet seems obvious, then why do so many young women in Europe and the USA not eat one? There are a number of answers to this question:

1 the food industry has confused people,
2 the customs of choosing, preparing and cooking food which were familiar to our grandmothers have been lost,
3 for many young women, the pace of life is such that cooking traditional meals competes with other priorities.

Those who believe that the problem of poor diet is merely the problem of lower socio-economic groups who eat junk food should call in at an expensive restaurant and see young executives eating steak and salad without starchy foods, in order to control their weight. The next chapter gives an insight into the diets of young women today.

PRE-CONCEPTION

Without doubt the balanced diet benefits both mother and baby, but its greatest benefits may come if it is begun before conception takes place. Increasingly, studies of humans, cattle and sheep are showing that the embryo is sensitive to the nutrition it receives and may be permanently and profoundly changed by it. This was discussed in the last chapter. The size of the mother's body at the time of conception has an important effect on the baby's birthweight. For example, large women

The size of the mother's body and her nutrient reserves at the time of conception have an important effect on the baby's birthweight.

have large babies, even if the egg was donated by a small woman and fertilised in a test tube. The baby does not depend only on what the mother eats each day, as that would render the baby too vulnerable to the mother becoming temporarily short of food or ill. After all, many mothers have long periods of sickness and loss of appetite during early pregnancy. Instead, the baby calls on the mother's nutrient reserves which are either in stores (iron, for example, is stored in the bone marrow, folic acid in the liver) or incorporated into the mother's muscle, bone and fat. These reserves need to be built up in the months and years before pregnancy.

WHAT IS A BALANCED DIET?

There is a young woman in my home town who lives on Pot Noodles – an instant pasta snack – and coffee. We are not expecting her to die. Her health is unremarkable and she maintains a responsible job. Her diet, however, will not meet the additional demands for nutrients that major illness or surgery may bring. She is unlikely to become a successful athlete. Her diet will not meet the challenges imposed by pregnancy. Pot Noodles alone are not a balanced diet.

A balanced diet is made up of food from five groups. They are:

1 **bread, other cereals and potatoes**
2 **fruit and vegetables**
3 **meat, fish and alternatives**
4 **milk and dairy foods**
5 **fats and sugary foods**

The following description accords with recommendations for a balanced diet generally accepted on both sides of the Atlantic. The nutrient content of individual foods is not described as it is not possible to build a diet by reference to tables of the amounts of nutrients in each of a long list of foods. There are many constituents of food about which we know little. Women achieved balance and variety in their diets long before such details were known and can readily do so again today.

1 Bread, other cereals and potatoes

These foods are rich in carbohydrates, broken down by the body into sugars, which supply half of the energy in the typical Western diet. However, bread, cereals and potatoes are more than sources of energy. They provide essential nutrients, including the B vitamins needed to generate the energy locked into carbohydrates. They are also useful sources of other nutrients such as folic acid. There is a mistaken belief that bread and potatoes make people fat, and some diets recommend their avoidance. The fact is that they are no more fattening than any other food eaten in excess. For example, a medium-sized potato provides 40 calories and a slice of bread 70 calories, while a 50g chocolate bar provides 250.

Breads, cereals and potatoes are filling and should be the basis of meals and snacks. They are the foundation on which a balanced diet is built.

Breads, cereals and potatoes are filling and should be the basis of meals and snacks. They are the foundation on which a balanced diet is built. Although some books about diet in pregnancy prescribe the numbers of daily servings of standard portions – for example, four tablespoonsful of rice – such prescriptions are unnecessary. An enjoyable, balanced and varied diet that meets all the needs of one individual can be created without weights and measures. How much bread, cereals and potatoes are needed is largely determined by a woman's energy requirements, a product of her body size and the amount of physical activity she carries out. This is discussed in more detail in the next chapter. In addition these foods supply important nutrients. Wholemeal bread and brown rice contain more nutrients than white bread and white rice because the outer layers of grains are nutrient-rich. Nevertheless, the refined foods remain good sources of nutrients and a balanced diet can still be achieved whatever choice is made.

2 Fruit and vegetables

Five servings of fruit and vegetables a day have become widely accepted as desirable. Although this recommendation comes from consideration of the needs of the general population, rather than the specific needs of pregnant women, there is no reason to challenge it. There is no prescription for the kind of fruit or vegetables or the balance of one to the other. But it provides a framework within which a desirable variety in fruit and vegetables can be achieved, and is attended by little risk of becoming over-weight because these foods are low in energy.

Fruit and vegetables contain many vitamins including folic acid, as well as minerals drawn from the soil. Though present in minute amounts, these are essential for a range of functions, including the transport of oxygen and the baby's growth. Fruit and vegetables are also a rich source of anti-oxidants. Even though it is essential for life, oxygen damages some molecules. After all, rust is the result of damage to metal by oxygen. In the body, cells are damaged by constant exposure to oxygen, so anti-oxidants in fruit and vegetables – such as vitamin C and carotenoids – are an important part of the body's protection against oxygen damage.

In a recent study of women's diets before and during pregnancy, green vegetables have been shown to increase babies' birthweights. Surprisingly, the effect seems to be greater than would be expected from the growth-promoting substances (such as folic acid) that they are known to contain. This could be explained by the presence of beneficial substances in fruit and vegetables that have not yet been identified, the existence of which could explain why the results of supplementing people's diets with single nutrients have had such disappointingly small benefits for their health. It therefore argues for eating different types of fruit and vegetables, an argument supported by the wide variation of vitamins and minerals known to be present in the different types.

It is important to note that some of the vitamins in fruit and vegetables are unstable, easily destroyed by storage, processing and during cooking. The degree of instability depends on the particular vitamin. Canning or drying reduces the vitamin content, though when vegetables are frozen, there are only small losses. Vitamin loss from vegetables can be minimised by using small amounts of water when boiling them, by steaming and by cooking for as short a time as possible. The guidelines suggest that out of the five daily portions, one can be fruit juice. Soft drinks like orangeade are not a substitute for orange juice as they are mostly water and sugar. Potatoes are not included under the term vegetables.

3 Meat, fish and alternatives

Meat is not an essential component of the human diet, but it has formed a significant part of it for thousands of years. Meat, fish, poultry, eggs, beans and lentils provide protein, though other foods such as bread and milk also contain protein. A serving of meat contains 20g of protein; a glass of milk contains 6g; two slices of bread contain 5g. Whereas carbohydrates are the body's energy source, proteins form the substance of the body, making up about one-sixth of its weight. Much of this is muscle, but there is also protein in the body's organs and in the skin. Proteins are also part of the body's transport system: like boats they carry nutrients, hormones and other messengers through the channels and canals of the body's fluid systems, linking the control centres in the brain to the cells and tissues they command.

Meat, fish, poultry and eggs each contain all of the essential amino acids, and the profile of amino acids in each of them is similar and close to what nutritional science regards as desirable.

As already described in Chapter 5, though seemingly fixed in their shape and size from one day to the next, the muscles of the body are in fact being continuously reconstructed or 'turned over', as the proteins in them are broken down and re-formed. This process is not fully efficient, which leads to a continual need for additional protein intake to make good the shortfall. Proteins are made up from amino acids, of which there are around twenty different kinds and, like the letters of the alphabet, they can be joined together in many different ways to give a rich vocabulary. Each makes a different contribution to the protein that includes it, with different functions and different capabilities. The amount of amino acids in the mother's bloodstream, and therefore available to the baby, will be influenced by the rate and scale of the mother's turnover as well as by her diet. Larger mothers, with more muscle and larger organs, can more readily make amino acids available to the baby, though naturally this will be modified by the types of food they eat. The mother's turnover and her diet work in harmony. The relative importance of either of them depends on circumstances. In the wartime famine in Holland the mothers' bodies were almost the only source of protein.

Some amino acids can be manufactured by the mother using other amino acids as scaffolding. Others, so-called essential amino acids, must be supplied by foods. If one of the essential amino acids is only present in the diet in small amounts, it will limit the usefulness of other amino acids. Meat, fish, poultry and eggs each contain all of the essential amino acids, and the profile of amino acids in each of them is similar and close to what nutritional science regards as desirable. A moment's reflection suggests that these four foods will inevitably be different in their content of other nutrients. Meat is mostly muscle, while an egg is designed to nourish a young bird without any additional supplementation while it develops. Meat is an important source of zinc and iron, red meat having more than white. Fish has less of these two minerals. Fish is a good and varied source of fatty acids, which are described below. Concerns about accumulation of heavy metals in certain fish can be set aside if a variety is eaten. Pulses (beans and lentils) are good sources of protein, though different types tend to be low in different amino acids. Once again, this argues for variety in the diet. A combination of pulses and cereals provides a full range of amino acids.

The experiences in the Scottish town showed that, unlike fruit and vegetables, there is an optimal intake of meat, fish and poultry. Although this optimum will have wide limits, high meat intakes during pregnancy are discouraged. Health education leaflets use phrases such as 'Eat in moderation'. Moderation, though in one sense unhelpful as advice, can be defined by common sense and custom. The diet in the Scottish town clearly went beyond common sense, in the pursuit of a single goal, the prevention of one disease.

Bread, cereals and potatoes are the foundation of a balanced diet. Pursuing the metaphor, the amount of meat and fish to be consumed must therefore depend on the foundations, in order to preserve a balance. The ideal balance of protein to carbohydrate is a ratio of approximately 1:2. Suppose a woman is eating four servings of the carbohydrate foods a day (in the language of dietetics a serving is around two slices of bread or three boiled potatoes). On this foundation the preferred balance would be one to two servings of meat, fish, poultry or eggs (a serving is a lamb chop, three slices of roast meat, a cod fillet, or four tablespoonsful of pulses). In the Scottish town the servings of meat, fish and eggs exceeded those of bread, cereals and potatoes in a ratio of 3:1, well outside the optimal range.

Bread, cereals and potatoes are the foundation of a balanced diet. Pursuing the metaphor, the amount of meat and fish to be consumed must therefore depend on the foundations, in order to preserve a balance.

Liver is not recommended in pregnancy because it contains excess vitamin A, which in large amounts may damage the baby. Aside from this there is no basis for recommending particular meats. The wide range of meat products available and their varying composition makes this impracticable.

4 Milk and dairy foods

Milk provides a complete source of nourishment for young animals. Little wonder, therefore, that it is a rich food. It is a major source of calcium, which is needed to make bone, and contains many other nutrients including protein and B vitamins. Bone is strong because calcium compounds are laid down on a protein scaffolding. Milk and milk products, such as cheese and yoghurt, provide around half the calcium in an average British diet and around three-quarters in the USA, and have been an important part of traditional diets since animal husbandry began.

During the period of pregnancy, the mother has to transfer around 30g (one ounce) of calcium to the baby. One might infer, therefore, that she needs to increase the calcium in her diet once she knows she is pregnant, especially in late pregnancy when much of bone growth occurs. However, if her diet is already adequate in calcium, once she becomes pregnant her body will adapt and make more calcium available to the baby, from the substantial reserves in her bones and by greater absorption from the intestines. Like muscle and the proteins within it, bone is in a constant state of flux, with calcium continuously being released and deposited. A woman with a good diet does not require extra calcium during pregnancy. More generally, pregnancy does not need to be attended by alteration to the varied and balanced diet that is appropriate before conception.

Although health messages about the possible links between dietary fat and heart disease have led to recommendations that skimmed milk is preferable to whole milk, there must be uncertainty as to whether this advice is wise for young women. Skimming removes more than fat: some vitamins are dissolved in the fat and therefore removed with it. Current recommendations are for several servings of dairy foods a day, a serving being either a glass of milk, a small pot of yoghurt or a piece of cheese. Soft mould-ripened cheeses such as Camembert and blue vein cheese are not recommended in pregnancy because they can contain high levels of the bacteria listeria. There is no such risk from hard cheeses and cottage cheese.

5 Fats and sugary foods

Meat, oily fish, dairy products, cooking oils and nuts are sources of fat. While carbohydrates are the baby's immediate source of energy, and proteins form a major part of the substance of its body, fat is used to make the walls which separate one cell from another. Towards the end of pregnancy the baby begins to accumulate fat, which serves as an energy store for the period after birth while milk feeding becomes established. Thereafter it builds up a second store, in preparation for weaning. Formed from chains of carbon atoms, fatty acids are the building blocks of fats. They also contain hydrogen, and the more hydrogen, the more 'saturated' the fatty acid is. Fatty acids with different levels of saturation and different lengths of carbon chain have different properties and different effects on the body. This once again argues for eating a variety of fatty foods. However, saturated fats have been linked to the development of heart disease and, though the evidence is inconclusive, general advice is to avoid large amounts of fatty foods with high saturated fat contents – by cutting off some of the fat on meat and not using excess spreads on

Fatty acids are important structural components of the baby's brain, so health messages about the suspected long-term dangers of fat consumption must not create a barrier to the baby receiving adequate fatty acids.

bread. Whereas there are only around twenty different amino acids, the range of fatty acids is much greater. Certain functions require particular fatty acids. Like amino acids, some of these can be manufactured by the mother, but others are 'essential' and must be supplied by food. Oily fish and many vegetable oils are good sources of essential fatty acids.

Like protein in muscle and calcium in bone, the body's fat stores are turned over each day. In women fat makes up about one-third of the body's weight. Although it is most apparent where it is stored under the skin, there are hidden stores in the cavities of the abdomen. While only about 1 per cent of a mother's fat stores is turned over every day, the size of the stores is such that the fatty acid composition of a mother's diet during pregnancy may only be of secondary importance. The composition of her fat will depend on her food in the months before pregnancy. Fatty acids are important structural components of the baby's brain, so health messages about the suspected long-term dangers of fat consumption must not create a barrier to the baby receiving adequate fatty acids. Fats in the food also bring with them vitamins A, D and E, which dissolve in fat but not water, and are therefore not present in large amounts in foods such as fruit and vegetables.

Some pre-cooked meals and processed foods are high in fat. Fish and chips, for example, contain a lot of fat. However, fish and chips were invented in Britain in 1870 and have been a staple part of the national diet ever since. No one advises a diet founded on fish and chips, but a diet based on the recommendations described here, in which fish and chips forms an occasional component, is appropriate. Fatty foods such as meat pies, burgers and crisps are palatable, which is why the food industry makes them in such quantity. A woman does not need to be unduly concerned about the fatty acid content of her diet if she is conforming to guidelines 1 to 4 described already. Returning to the woman eating four servings of carbohydrate food a day, the one to two servings of meat, fish, poultry or eggs, and the several servings of dairy products, will give her baby what it needs. Additional fats from foods such as crisps and other snacks are unnecessary.

Sugary foods, such as cakes, biscuits, chocolate bars and sweetened drinks, are also palatable, but should be occasional foods. Added sugar does not bring with it anything that is useful to the baby except energy. By contrast, bread, cereals and potatoes are the main immediate sources of energy and bring with them a wide range of nutrients.

ANYONE CAN DO IT

A varied and balanced diet is based on simple principles. A little knowledge, no more than has been set out in the previous pages, can enable anyone to achieve one. The secret does not lie in exotic foods, in reading the food labels or in calculating the nutrient content of foods. A good diet is not built on tables of the mineral content of all known vegetables. In a diet which contains a variety of foods calculation is unnecessary. With knowledge of the principles, prescribed daily servings are unnecessary beyond those that ensure a reasonable balance of protein and carbohydrate foods, and an adequate amount of fruit, vegetables and dairy products.

Our forebears learned the principles of a good diet from the food that they grew, from the varying food that each season brought and from the need to store essential foods to see the family through the winter. New dietary habits developed when our parents and grandparents left the countryside, when natural food was replaced by manufactured food, and when busy town dwellers no longer had the time to prepare and cook food. It is a paradox of our times that so many people eat so badly when food is more widely available than ever in the past – for example, when fresh peas from Ecuador and strawberries from Kenya are available at Christmas. At the National Institute of Health in Washington the cost of food in the canteen depends solely on its weight: what kind of food is on the plate is irrelevant, quality takes second place to quantity. In the next chapter the principles of a varied and balanced diet are translated into meals.

7

Achieving a Balanced Diet

In a recent study in England 8000 women between the ages of twenty and thirty-four completed a diary of the food they ate during one twenty-four-hour period. The diary was delivered to them at home by a nurse who explained how to record all food and drinks taken. These women's willingness to put their diets on record has given us a unique insight into the food habits of young women in Britain today.

The women came from all walks of life: some were married; some lived with a partner; some were single, but none of them was pregnant. Some went out to work while some remained at home. Half of them had children, one-third were smokers, one-quarter had had higher education. Some diaries showed that a balanced and varied diet can be fitted into a wide variety of lifestyles, and is readily achievable. Others showed that while many young women's diets do not meet the recommendations made in the last chapter, they could readily be made to do so. Five of their diaries are presented here, though the names and personal details have been changed.

In the diaries the following symbols are used for the five food categories.

① Bread, other cereals and potatoes
② Fruit and vegetables
③ Meat, fish and alternatives
④ Milk and dairy foods
⑤ Fats and sugary foods

The diets described in four of the five diaries do not follow the guidelines for a balanced diet in various ways. Of course, they represent only a snapshot of a diet that may change from day to day. The women, however, were also asked about their diets over the past three months and their one-day diaries broadly reflected their habitual patterns of eating. You are invited to appraise these diets one by one and identify where they depart from the guidelines. Specific comments on each diet are given below the diary.

HOLLY is twenty-one years old. At school she achieved a good level of education and now works full-time as an administrative assistant. She is married.

Tuesday 16 December

7.30 a.m.	Bowl of breakfast cereal with milk ① ④	Glass orange juice ②
10.45 a.m.		Glass orange juice ②
11.40 a.m.		Instant hot chocolate ④ ⑤
1.20 p.m.	White bread roll with cheese and onion ① ④	Blackcurrant cordial (with added vitamin C) ⑤
2.40 p.m.	Chocolate bar ⑤	
7.30 p.m.	Cheese and tomato pizza ① ④ Chips ① 2 biscuits ⑤	Glass lemonade ⑤
8.30 p.m.		Glass lemonade ⑤

Holly's diet consisted of three main meals, each based on bread, cereals or potatoes, as recommended. On that day Holly had only two glasses of orange juice and no other fruit or vegetables – the piece of onion in her cheese roll is too little to count, as is the tomato in the pizza. She has an adequate three servings of dairy products. Holly recorded that she was taking iron tablets on prescription. Whatever the reason that she has become short of iron, her diet is not helping. The rich sources of iron include meat and green vegetables, and Holly did not eat either of them, though she did eat bread and breakfast cereals, both of which contribute to the iron in food. This is an unbalanced diet.

LUCY is twenty-five years old. She is married with twins aged three years. She works part-time in a florist's shop.

Sunday 22 March

10 a.m.	4 slices white toast with low-fat spread and marmalade ① ⑤	Glass orange juice ②
2.15 p.m.	Bag of crisps ⑤ 6 pieces of French bread with low-fat spread ① ⑤	Glass orangeade ⑤
6 p.m.	6 slices roast pork ③ 8 roast potatoes and gravy ①	Glass water
7 p.m.	3 pieces chocolate ⑤	Glass Coke ⑤
8.30 p.m.	5 pieces chocolate ⑤	
Midnight	3 slices white bread with low-fat spread ① ⑤	Glass Coke ⑤

Although this is a structured diet based on three meals, it is a curious one. Lucy cooked a main meal of roast pork with roast potatoes and gravy, but she did not cook any vegetables or have another course. She ate no dairy products. Through the day she ate the equivalent of ten slices of bread. These, together with the potatoes and chocolate, laid the foundations for a high-energy diet on that day, amounting to around 2500 calories. She recorded that on average she watches television for four and a half hours every day and she takes no strenuous exercise. She weighs 69 kilograms (152 pounds) and, given this and her sedentary lifestyle, her average energy requirement is around 2100 calories each day.

If her diet on that day was typical, she will inevitably become overweight unless she takes more exercise.

DEBORAH is thirty years old and a single mother living with her three-year-old son. She is currently dieting to lose weight. She is overweight.

Friday 6 April

7.30 a.m.		Mug herbal tea
8.30 a.m.	Bowl of breakfast cereal with skimmed milk ① ④	
10 a.m.		Glass water
12 noon	Cup of instant soup (sold as 98 per cent fat free) Wholemeal roll ① Pre-packed cold chicken slices with green salad ③ ② 1 pot Weightwatchers' yoghurt ④	
1 p.m.		Mug white coffee ④
2 p.m.		Mug white coffee ④
3.30 p.m.	2 biscuits ⑤	Mug white coffee ④
5 p.m.	Roast chicken without skin ③ Baked potato and skin ① Fresh boiled swede, carrots and broccoli ②	
6 p.m.	Small chocolate bar ⑤	Cup tea ④
8 p.m.		Mug white coffee ④
9 p.m.		Mug white coffee ④

Deborah's diet centred on three meals, at each of which she ate bread, cereals or potatoes, as is recommended. Although she had four servings of fresh vegetables and salad, she ate no fresh fruit on that day. She ate chicken twice rather than eating some other form of meat or fish for one of her meals. Perhaps because she is dieting she largely avoided high-fat foods – drinking skimmed milk, using no butter or spread, cutting the skin off the roast chicken and limiting herself to a small bar of chocolate and two biscuits. Such a diet may provide an inadequate variety of fats which, as has been described, are essential for the body's health.

FIONA is twenty-seven years old, and lives with her husband and two children, aged three years and six months.

Tuesday 4 December

9 a.m.	Slice white bread with spread ① ⑤	Mug white decaffeinated coffee ④
10.15 a.m.	Grapes ② Orange ②	
10.35 a.m.	3 chocolate biscuits ⑤	Mug white decaffeinated coffee ④
12.10 p.m.	Small chocolate bar ⑤	
12.30 p.m.	Vegetable chilli with mixed beans, carrots, courgettes, onions, mushrooms, red peppers ② Couscous ①	
2 p.m.	3 peppermints ⑤	Summer fruits drink ⑤
2.05 p.m.		Mug tea ④
3.30 p.m.	2 mince pies ⑤	Mug decaffeinated tea ④
5 p.m.	Satsuma and half pear ②	

6.45 p.m.	Roast chicken with gravy ③ Roast potatoes ① Carrots ② Green beans ② Peas ②	
7.10 p.m.		Glass milk ④
9.10 p.m.	3 scoops chocolate ice cream ⑤	
10 p.m.		Hot chocolate drink ④ ⑤

Fiona eats a varied and balanced diet.

JANE is a graduate aged twenty-four years who works as an office manager and shares a flat with her partner.

Thursday 20 August

8 a.m.	Breakfast cereal with milk ① ④ 2 slices toast with spread ① ⑤	Cup tea ④
1.30 p.m.	Cheese sandwich ① ④ Packet crisps ⑤	Glass orange juice ②
6 p.m.	Roast potatoes ① Cauliflower ② Cheese sauce ④ Vegetarian sausage ③ Quorn nuggets ③ Yorkshire pudding ① Bowl of instant milk dessert ④ ⑤ Few sweets ⑤	2 glasses wine
9 p.m.	Packet crisps ⑤	

Jane is a vegetarian. Her diet is built around three meals, each of which is based on bread, cereals or potatoes. While many of the diets of vegetarian women in the study were varied and balanced, Jane's lacks fruit. On the day of her diary she substituted processed food (vegetarian sausage and nuggets) for other meat alternatives, such as pulses (beans, lentils). Processed foods are a useful adjunct to the modern diet because they enable busy people to prepare appetising meals quickly; but over-reliance on them brings the risk of unknown deficiencies or imbalances.

IMPEDIMENTS TO A BALANCED DIET

Many of the diets of the young women who helped in the study lacked variety or were unbalanced. Why? The reason most commonly given for not eating a better diet was that there was insufficient time in the day to prepare and cook food. This may be a perception rather than a reality, because people usually make time to do things they regard as important. Another commonly given reason was that to many people a balanced diet was less palatable than an unbalanced one. However, the next section of this chapter demonstrates that a diet can become balanced without removing favourite foods. As described in Chapter 6, variety is important because not all the nutrients present in foods have been identified and variety of food is a protection against deficiency. Although presenting a family with new dishes runs the risk of rejection, many women's three-month diaries show that they have settled into a diet with too little variety.

Disturbingly, lack of knowledge about food is not widely perceived to be a barrier to eating a better diet. In a recent survey, 70 per cent of people across Europe believed they were eating a healthy diet. Paradoxically, many people's lack of knowledge of what constitutes a balanced diet coexists with information about food being more widely available than ever before. One source of confusion is that for many young women the phrases 'healthy eating' and 'dieting to make me slim' are interchangeable. Another source of confusion is the remarkable range of foods now available. A supermarket offers overwhelming choices.

In Britain one in four people say that price is an important barrier to eating a better diet; in Italy only one in ten people say the same. This is curious because many of the meals in the unbalanced diets in the diaries were more expensive than the meals that contributed to a balanced diet. The excess of sugary foods in many diets contributes little nutritionally. To an Italian, price may not be a barrier to a good diet because eating is culturally more important than it is in Britain, a social occasion rather than simply refuelling, something worth spending money on. In Britain today it takes a certain confidence to select fresh food, prepare it and cook it, whereas in southern Europe it is second nature to many people. Because of the more severe climate in northern Europe, the long winters when in the past potatoes and occasional meat were the only food, the culture of a varied diet and the cooking traditions that go with it have been slower to develop. The average Briton still eats over half his or her bodyweight in chips (French fries) each year.

Undoubtedly health messages have confused the public. Few of the women's food diaries included a boiled egg for breakfast. Twenty-five years ago, 'Go to work on an egg' was a familiar slogan. Before the Second World War, campaigns to reduce the incidence of tuberculosis rightly extolled the virtue of dairy products, but after the war the hypothesis that fat in the diet caused heart disease led to an onslaught on the dairy industry. In her book, *Food in History*, Reay Tannahill writes about the 'anti' campaigns of the last thirty years – campaigns that were anti-saturated fats, sugar and salt. 'The public were soon persuaded to change to margarine (or, later, reduced-fat spreads) in place of butter, semi-skimmed in place of full-cream milk, chicken in place of red meat, and so on.' She continues that 'the "anti" campaigners were so successful that it led to a number of dangerous developments, including an insistence on lean meat that in the early days led to much metabolic tinkering of farm animals. New labelling laws and the imaginative presentation techniques of the supermarkets seem to imply a guarantee of respectability, so that the good intentions of consumers are undermined. Labels such as "healthy", "natural", "low-fat", "bal-anced", "sugar-free" are taken on trust and influence decisions.

Such labels are not to be found in the fresh food markets of Continental Europe. It is, in fact, usually impossible for the consumer to tell whether the meat in a 'ready meal' has come from a conventionally raised animal or one that had been defatted with the aid of chemicals, or intensively reared on antibiotics.'

The women's diaries give us an insight into busy lives: the need to balance the responsibilities of work, home and childcare. The diets of many women are conditioned by lack of time, lack of knowledge, the desire to lose weight, the cost of food, lack of traditional cooking skills and the confusion brought by the 'anti' campaigners on the one side and the 'healthy eating' lobby on the other. Does change have to wait on legislation or a change in heart by the food industry? The next section describes how a few simple alterations to the day's food can transform an unbalanced diet lacking variety into a varied and balanced one.

BALANCING UP THE DIETS

Four of the five diaries shown above did not meet the recommendations for a balanced diet. They are now presented again with some simple suggestions that would result in a balanced diet and, unless it is needed because of extra physical demands, without any substantial increase in calories.

HOLLY

7.30 a.m.	Bowl of breakfast cereal with milk ① ④	Glass orange juice ②
10.45 a.m.	*Fresh pear* ②	Glass orange juice ②
11.40 a.m.		Instant hot chocolate ④ ⑤
1.20 p.m.	White bread roll with cheese and onion ① ④ *Apple* ②	Blackcurrant cordial (with added vitamin C) ⑤
2.40 p.m.	~~Chocolate bar ⑤~~ *Dried apricots* ②	

122

| 7.30 p.m. | Cheese and tomato pizza ① ④ *with added green peppers and mushrooms* ② *Baked beans* ② Chips ① 2 biscuits ⑤ | Glass lemonade ⑤ |
| 8.30 p.m. | | Glass lemonade ⑤ |

Holly ate no fruit, and a pear and an apple have been added. She recorded that she was taking iron tablets on prescription. She did not eat either meat or green vegetables, the rich sources of iron. Her diet has therefore been reinforced with green peppers, baked beans and dried apricots. She does not eat meat because she is a vegetarian. Beans and lentils are good sources of protein and many vegetarians use a variety of them in their diets.

LUCY

10 a.m.	4 slices white toast with low-fat spread and marmalade ① ⑤	Glass orange juice ②
2.15 p.m.	Bag of crisps ⑤ *Apple* ② 6 pieces of French bread with low-fat spread ① ⑤ *Cottage cheese* ④	Glass orangeade ⑤
6 p.m.	6 slices roast pork ③ 3 slices roast pork ③ 8 roast potatoes 4 roast potatoes ① gravy ① *Frozen peas* ② *Broccoli* ② *Yoghurt* ④	Glass water
7 p.m.	3 pieces chocolate ⑤	Glass Coke ⑤

| 8.30 p.m. | 5 pieces chocolate ⑤ *Banana* ② | |
| Midnight | 3 slices white bread with low fat spread ① ⑥ | Glass Coke ⑤ |

Lucy's calorie intake has been reduced to around 2100 by reducing the servings of roast pork and potatoes, substituting a banana for chocolate in the evening and removing the snack at midnight. She now has vegetables with her main meal of roast pork, two servings of dairy products and some fresh fruit.

DEBORAH

7.30 a.m.		Mug herbal tea
8.30 a.m.	Bowl of breakfast cereal with skimmed milk ① ④	
10 a.m.		Glass water
12 noon	Cup of instant soup (sold as 98 per cent fat free) Wholemeal roll ① Pre-packed cold chicken slices ③ *Tinned tuna* ③ Green salad ② 1 pot Weightwatchers' yoghurt ④	
1 p.m.		Mug white coffee ④
2 p.m.		Mug white coffee ④
3.30 p.m.	2 biscuits ⑤	Mug white coffee ④
5 p.m.	Roast chicken without skin ③ Baked potato and skin ① Fresh boiled swede, carrots and broccoli ② *Fresh fruit salad* ②	

6 p.m.	Small chocolate bar ⑤	Cup tea ④
8 p.m.		Mug white coffee ④
9 p.m.		Mug white coffee ④

Deborah now has fruit in her diet and a variety of fats from meat and fish.

JANE

8 a.m.	Breakfast cereal with milk ① ④ 2 slices toast with spread ① ⑤	Cup tea ④
1.30 p.m.	Cheese sandwich ① ④ *Apple* ② Packet crisps ⑤	Glass orange juice ②
6 p.m.	Roast potatoes ① *Peas* ② Cauliflower ② Cheese sauce ④ Vegetarian sausage ③ Quorn nuggets ③ Yorkshire pudding ① *2 kiwi fruits* ② Bowl of instant milk dessert ④ ⑤ Few sweets ⑤	2 glasses wine
9 p.m.	~~Packet crisps ⑤~~	

Jane's diet now includes fruit. On this one day her diet remains over-reliant on processed vegetarian food and the substitution of beans or lentils would redress this.

FOOD STORES FOR BUSY PEOPLE

Three years ago a well-known photographer was commissioned to carry out a study of the contents of ordinary household fridges in the homes of seventy young women in an English city. She produced a compelling set of photographs. Some fridges were empty, except for perhaps a tub of margarine, a packet of processed chicken, or a bar of chocolate. At the other extreme were fridges packed with fresh vegetables, salad, milk and butter. Between these two extremes most fridges contained a few jars of pickles, a tub or two of spreads, sandwich fillings, some packaged vegetables and bowls of leftovers. The photographs are startling visual evidence of the paucity of fresh foods in the diets of many Englishwomen.

Had the photographer visited the women's kitchen cupboards and larders it is likely the picture would have been similar. Keeping stores of certain foods makes it easier to achieve balanced diets of the kind that have been presented. The following are suggestions for the kind of stored foods which will allow a varied and balanced diet.

Freezer	Fridge	Kitchen cupboard
Garden peas, green beans and other vegetables Bread, rolls Pizzas/pizza bases Fish, fish fingers, fishcakes Chicken, sausages, mince, meat substitutes	Milk Butter/spread Eggs Cheeses Salad vegetables Other vegetables Yoghurt, fromage frais, crème fraiche Fruit juice Salad dressings and sauces Potatoes Cold meats and bacon Tomato purée	Fresh fruit Onions and garlic Pasta Rice Breakfast cereals Canned fish Tinned tomatoes, beans and soup Custard powder Cooking oils Sugar Spices, stock cubes Dried herbs Preserves Dried pulses, lentils Flour

THE OTHER FOOD STORES

This is but one of the larders that will nourish the baby. The other is the mother's body. At the time of conception and through pregnancy the baby calls on the reserves of protein and fat which are incorporated into the mother's muscle and fat, and which are released into her blood through daily 'turnover'. Calcium is released from her bones, iron from her bone marrow, folic acid from her liver. This second larder is the product of the mother's growth from childhood. Chapter 5 described how even the mother's birthweight influenced the birthweight of her baby. Nevertheless the larder can be stocked up by a varied and balanced diet in the months before conception.

The realisation that a mother's capacity to nourish her baby is established during her early life is not new. Edward Mellanby became famous through his discoveries that rickets, which deforms the bones of young children, was due to nutritional deficiency. He induced the disease in dogs by feeding them on porridge and cured it by giving them cod liver oil, which was later found to contain vitamin D. He wrote that 'it is certain that the significance of correct nutrition in child bearing does not begin in pregnancy itself or even in the adult female before pregnancy. It looms large as soon as a female child is born and indeed in its intrauterine life.' Others have elaborated on this theme. The anthropologist, Ashley Montague, wrote, 'A mother's good nutrition over her whole lifetime results in the superior development of her own body. If she has grown normally from her own pre-natal days her own organs will be splendidly equal to the job of nurturing her child; if not they may be less able. On the other hand, a young woman whose own background has been poverty-stricken or deprived can, by providing a good diet for herself and her child, compensate to a large extent for her deficiencies.'

The next chapter discusses childhood growth, an understanding of which is important both because it determines part of a mother's ability to nourish her baby and because the baby's own growth in childhood will contribute importantly to its lifelong health.

8

A Child's Growth

THE EVOLUTION OF HUMAN GROWTH

Human beings are unique. We walk on two legs and have large brains. We can breed in any season, in any climate: our material culture protects us from the environment. Our path of growth is different from other animals, yet it is still governed by the processes which governed the growth of our ancestors. Through our immediate ancestors, apes and monkeys, we evolved our large head size at birth, the product of novel modifications of the mammalian placenta and our deferment of sexual maturity until the growth of the brain is more or less complete. Through them also we evolved our rapid spurt in growth during adolescence and we share with them the custom of usually having only one baby per pregnancy. From our more remote ancestors, in common with all other mammals, we acquired our custom of investing in our offspring after they are born. Our skeleton and musculature are based on a mammalian pattern of growth, which produces a body able to move quickly and flexibly, using efficient muscles and special joints. Human illnesses in later life often originate in association with early growth. Growth is moulded by the environment. Growth responds to the environment through a blueprint laid down in our distant evolutionary past.

THE MOTHER'S WEIGHT AND SHAPE

Around the world the size and shape of young women varies widely and is changing rapidly, something which must have profound consequences for the growth of babies. The average weights of young women of a comparable age are 41 kilograms

CHART 1: BODY MASS INDEX CALCULATOR

Height in feet & inches	Weight in stones															Height in cm
	6	7	8	9	10	11	12	13	14	15	16	17	18	19	20	
4'3"	23	26	30	34	38	42	45	49	53	57	61	64	68	72	76	130
4'4"	22	25	29	33	36	40	44	47	51	55	58	62	66	69	73	132
4'5"	21	25	28	32	35	39	42	46	49	53	56	60	63	67	70	135
4'6"	20	24	27	30	34	37	41	44	47	51	54	57	61	64	68	137
4'7"	20	23	26	29	33	36	39	42	46	49	52	55	59	62	65	140
4'8"	19	22	25	28	31	35	38	41	44	47	50	53	56	60	63	142
4'9"	18	21	24	27	30	33	36	39	42	45	48	51	55	58	61	145
4'10"	18	20	23	26	29	32	35	38	41	44	47	50	53	56	59	147
4'11"	17	20	23	25	28	31	34	37	40	42	45	48	51	54	57	150
4'12"	16	19	22	25	27	30	33	36	38	41	44	46	49	52	55	152
5'1"	16	19	21	24	26	29	32	34	37	40	42	45	48	50	53	155
5'2"	15	18	20	23	26	28	31	33	36	38	41	44	46	49	51	157
5'3"	15	17	20	22	25	27	30	32	35	37	40	42	45	47	50	160
5'4"	14	17	19	22	24	26	29	31	34	36	38	41	43	46	48	163
5'5"	14	16	19	21	23	26	28	30	33	35	37	40	42	44	47	165
5'6"	14	16	18	20	23	25	27	29	32	34	36	38	41	43	45	168
5'7"	13	15	18	20	22	24	26	29	31	33	35	37	39	42	44	170
5'8"	13	15	17	19	21	23	26	28	30	32	34	36	38	40	43	173
5'9"	12	14	17	19	21	23	25	27	29	31	33	35	37	39	41	175
5'10"	12	14	16	18	20	22	24	26	28	30	32	34	36	38	40	178
5'11"	12	14	16	18	20	21	23	25	27	29	31	33	35	37	39	180
5'12"	11	13	15	17	19	20	23	24	26	28	30	32	34	36	38	183
6'1"	11	13	15	17	18	20	22	23	25	28	30	31	33	35	37	185
6'2"	11	13	14	16	18	20	22	23	25	27	29	31	32	34	36	188
	38	44	51	57	64	70	76	83	89	95	102	108	114	121	127	

Weight in kilograms

(90 pounds) in rural India, 61 kilograms (134 pounds) in Britain and 64 kilograms (141 pounds) in the USA. Within Western countries, however, women have a remarkable range of body weights. This is apparent in adolescent girls. A recent study of sixteen-year-old girls in Britain found that their weights ranged from 35 to 97 kilograms (77 to 214 pounds).

Weight measures fatness, muscularity and height. To assess fatness it is usual to relate weight to height to produce a measure called the body mass index:

$$\text{BMI} = \frac{\text{weight in kilograms}}{(\text{height in metres})^2}$$

The body mass indices of the sixteen-year-old British girls ranged from 15 to 35. A body mass below 18 is regarded as thin. Though this is average among young women in rural India where many girls are poorly nourished from childhood, in Western countries many women are as slim as this by choice. Currently a person is defined as overweight if their body mass index is above 25 and obese if it exceeds 30. Although a high body mass index may also be a result of muscularity – Olympic sprinters have high body mass indices – it provides a good guide to fatness for most people. Chart 1 on the previous page allows a woman to calculate her body mass index based on her weight and height. Current advice is that women with a body mass index below 18 could usefully gain weight, provided they do so on a balanced diet. The problems associated with obesity in young women are well known and the period before pregnancy may be an appropriate one in which to try to achieve a healthy weight.

Different women store fat in different places at any level of overall fatness and fat stored in different parts of the body has different actions. For example, fat on the arms, below the shoulder or above the hips makes different amounts of oestrogen, while overweight women whose fat has accumulated on the abdomen tend to be resistant to the effects of insulin, which raises the sugar levels in their blood and hence predisposes them to diabetes, and may even make their babies excessively fat. In contrast, for women whose fat is stored on their hips, often described as 'pear-shaped' rather than 'apple-shaped', the implications of being overweight are less serious.

In Europe mothers gain around 12 kilograms (26 pounds) in weight during pregnancy. Of this, 7.7 kilograms (17 pounds) is due to increase in their fat, fluid, womb and breast tissue. Mothers store around 3 kilograms (7 pounds) of extra fat in the first half of pregnancy. This provides an energy store for the second half of pregnancy when the baby's need for energy is greatest and when it is building up its own fat stores in preparation for birth. Accumulation of fat in unusual places, such as on the back or thighs, is a normal response to pregnancy. The effects of thinness – low body mass index – at the time of conception can be partly offset by rapid weight gain in pregnancy, although the baby's weight still tends to remain below average. The American Institute of Medicine recommends that women with a body mass index below 19.8 should gain between 12.5 and 18 kg (28–40 pounds) during pregnancy. For those with a body mass index between 19.8 and 26, the recommendation is for 11.5–16 kg (25–35 pounds). Although these are the recommendations, weight gain in pregnancy is difficult to control, and a woman who is not obese and who eats a balanced diet may be best guided by her appetite.

We now know that women who are thin when they become pregnant tend to have offspring that are not only small at birth but have an altered metabolism for life. While Mao Tse-tung was camped with his army in the Fragrant Hills, waiting to enter Beijing and complete his victory over Chiang Kai-shek, work at a hospital in the city was continuing undisturbed. The Peking Union Medical College Hospital was brought from the London Missionary Society by the Rockefeller Foundation in 1920. The Foundation's vision was to create a school where the brightest of China's medical students could be trained. Doctors were brought from the USA and Europe to teach them, and a modern hospital was established. As part of their obstetric training the students attended the delivery room and were required to make detailed observations on each newborn baby. These included taking the baby's footprints and making drawings of the placenta, in ink, showing both its surface and its appearance from the side. These were added to the copious notes which were begun when the mothers first came to the hospital in early pregnancy, and which included their heights and weights.

Around the time China's Civil War came to an end in 1949, 600 babies were born in the hospital. They were born and were lost, disappearing into the new Communist world of a billion people, living through famine and the Cultural Revolution, before settling again in Beijing where, a few years ago, they were traced by Chinese researchers wishing to examine them and link their health to their appearance and size at birth. As expected, those who had been thin or stunted at birth had higher blood pressures and their bodies handled sugar differently. They were at risk of hypertension and diabetes. Those born to mothers with a low body mass index were at especially high risk of diabetes because they were insulin-resistant. This effect of the mother being thin was not simply the result of her tendency to have a small baby.

A direct link between thin mothers and defective handling of sugar by their babies has been found elsewhere – in the Scottish towns, in the Dutch famine, in India – and it is not extreme thinness that causes this, but thinness at levels encouraged by parts of the fashion industry.

A CHILD'S GROWTH: THREE QUESTIONS

The maps of England and Wales discussed in Chapter 1 led to the conclusion that two kinds of processes underlie heart disease: one associated with prosperity, which leads to rising epidemics of the disease as countries become Westernised and more affluent; the other associated with poverty, which makes people living in poorer conditions in Western countries more vulnerable to the disease. The Hertfordshire studies (Chapter 2) suggested that the influence of poor living conditions is mediated through poor nutrition and growth in the womb, and by poor growth during infancy. This predisposes people to disease because it leads to reduced capacity in organs such as the kidney, less efficient function in key systems such as that which controls the amount of sugar in the blood, and because it makes people more susceptible to biological and psychosocial stresses in later life. The studies in Helsinki (Chapter 4) and elsewhere suggested that the influence of prosperity is mediated through accelerated 'compensatory' increase in weight after the age of one year. Together, these studies pose three questions:

1 Why do some infants fail to thrive?
2 Why do some children who were small at birth or at one year of age put on weight rapidly in childhood?
3 Why should rapid weight gain lead to disease?

THE LESS DEMANDING CHILD

During infancy, babies grow rapidly so that by the age of one year they have added another 50 per cent to their birth length and have more than doubled their weight. The rate of growth, however, slows progressively during early childhood. From three years until puberty the child continues to grow at a slow though relatively constant rate of around five centimetres in height per year. The growth of most organs follows that of the body as a whole. The brain is an exception: it grows in advance of the body. By around seven years the head has reached about 80 per cent of its final size, whereas length is only 65 per cent. After seven years there is a small spurt in the rate of the body's growth that heralds the onset of puberty, when the adolescent growth spurt occurs. Girls usually begin their adolescent growth spurt at an earlier age than boys. Whereas girls increase their fat mass, boys increase their muscle mass and may even lose fat. It is a general phenomenon among mammals that the female lays down more fat than the male. It prepares her for the demands of pregnancy. Although boys and girls are of similar height before puberty, boys are taller when growth ceases because their adolescent growth spurt occurs later and they are therefore taller when it begins. Their growth spurt is also more intense.

One measure of the slowing of growth after infancy is that whereas the infant allocates 23 per cent of its energy to growth, the two-year-old allocates only 6 per cent. One possible advantage of this is that it helps to maintain the child's demand for food at relatively low levels and the child is less of an economic burden on the parents. Even so, there are many elderly Chinese people alive today who remember the day when, in hard times, their parents were forced to give them away so they could be fed. Girls were more often given away than boys, because they were less highly valued. A child's slow growth may also be linked to humans' high energy needs. Partly because of our large brains, at any body size we require more energy than most other mammals of the same size and the benefits of slow growth may therefore be greater.

A growing child needs energy for four main activities: staying alive, growing, keeping warm and moving. The first of these usually requires the most energy. The extent of this requirement, which in humans is called the basal metabolic rate, varies widely between individuals and is mainly determined by four organs, the brain, liver, heart and kidney. Although they represent only 6 per cent of the total weight of the body they require 65 per cent of the energy needed to stay alive. In contrast, muscle represents 30 per cent of body weight but makes a relatively small contribution to basal metabolism. Different pathways of growth lead to differences in the relative size of different organs and therefore to different basal metabolic energy requirements throughout life. This may be one of the factors through which, in periods of starvation, some people perish while others survive.

INFERIOR STOCK

The school doctors in Helsinki who measured the children's growth every six months did so because it was a simple way of characterising their well-being. Children who are undernourished, unwell or stressed in other ways – as are more than half the children alive in the world today – grow slowly and become stunted and thin. Mankind has known for thousands of years that undernutrition reduces the growth of animals; the scientific literature is enormous. Surprisingly, however, the link between poor living conditions and poor growth in humans only became accepted relatively recently. Edwin Chadwick, the British social reformer, was one of the first people to use growth measurements to illustrate the poor conditions under which children lived. His 'Report on the employment of Children in Factories', which led to the Factories' Regulation Act of 1833, cited the low heights and weights of children working in factories as evidence of the dreadful conditions in which they worked.

Until the last century there was a strong hereditarian school of thought. In his book, *Natural Inheritance*, published in 1889, Francis Galton proposed that height was inherited because an individual's height was related to that of his or her parents. In arguments that resonate with those we hear today, maintaining that our health is primarily determined by our inheritance, some people went on to propose that inheritance was the main determinant of human form and function. Poor children were stunted, thin and weak because they came from genetically inferior stock. Therefore there was no compelling reason to improve their lot – rather, as the statistician Karl Pearson argued, the weakling infants born in their thousands in the industrial towns of northern Britain should be allowed to perish, in order to maintain the physical quality of the nation.

However, Pearson was confusing the effects of genetic variation on growth with the effects of environmental conditions within the lifetime of an individual. His eugenic arguments faltered when, in the course of prolonged and bitter disputes, it was pointed out that in the northern towns, children and young adults had high death rates at every age, and the concept that inferior stock were being weeded out by high death rates during infancy, thereby enhancing the fitness of the surviving group of children, must be erroneous.

Around this time a different argument on the same theme was being fought in the USA. Hereditarians believed that physically inferior people from southern and eastern Europe, who were migrating into America in large numbers, would bring about a physical deterioration of Americans and that their intermarriage with Anglo-Saxons would weaken the stock for many generations. Franz Boas, an anthropologist born and trained in Germany, championed the anti-hereditarian cause. In a famous study of immigrant families in New York, he demonstrated that those children born in America were taller and heavier than their parents had been at the same age, and differently shaped as well. He ascribed it to the better nutrition and health of children in America, and concluded that the environment had a major influence on growth. This conclusion, now generally accepted, collided with the strongly held view that human types and races are fixed. Notwithstanding his correct scientific conclusion, the hereditarians and eugenicists campaigned successfully for a reduction in migration quotas from south and eastern Europe. It takes a while for scientific orthodoxies to yield to new scientific evidence, especially if the argument is based on a synthesis of biological information, like the origins of heart disease, as opposed to reductionist research like the structure of DNA, which can be readily demonstrated beyond question.

Boas continued to fight the idea that immigrants from poor countries were genetically destined to remain inferior for many generations. He went on to study their tempo of growth. The importance of rates of growth had already been proposed in a famous book by the mathematician, naturalist and Greek scholar, D'Arcy Thompson. *On Growth and Form*, published in 1917, is still read today: 'To say that children of a given age vary in the rate at which they are growing would seem to be a more fundamental statement than that they vary in the size to which they have grown.' Boas pointed out that immigrants' children born in the USA became physically different from how their parents had been at the same age within a year or so of birth. The greatest differences between parents and children were in families in which the parents grew up in their country of origin, while the children were born after the parents had reached the USA.

CHILDREN'S RESPONSE TO MALNUTRITION

Boas's observations on the growth of American immigrants have been replicated in other children who migrated into countries where their nutrition and health improved. Human growth is environmentally sensitive and responds to malnutrition, chronic illness, poor living conditions and stress. In Hertfordshire, a relatively affluent county in southern England, the growth of babies between birth and one year varied according to the family's circumstances. Even so crude an index of living conditions as the 'rateable value' of the houses (i.e. their value for taxation purposes) was linked to the growth rates of the infants living in them. Infants in homes in the highest tax band were more than a pound (0.5 kg) heavier at one year than those in homes in the lowest band. Karl Pearson, pursuing his hereditarian theories, studied the records of a child welfare clinic in a poor industrial town in the north of Britain around 1920. At one year of age the babies weighed on average only 16 pounds (7 kg) compared with 22 pounds (10 kg) in Hertfordshire at the same time.

In some Third World countries such as India, body weight is already low at birth. However, in others, such as in Africa, it is only after the first six months that children's weight gain begins to diminish in comparison with Western children. This may coincide with weaning when the infant diet is changed from breast milk to high-starch, low-protein food. By three years of age the size of the Third World child has fallen far below that of Western children. Thereafter it grows at a similar rate, but the deficit persists.

The experiences of immigrants illustrate how the growth of humans and other animals responds to adverse conditions. Slowing of growth is one response, another is delay in the final maturation of the skeleton, thereby allowing growth to continue for longer, and a third is to delay sexual maturation, the onset of puberty, thereby delaying the adolescent growth spurt. Those lizards in the mountains of southern France do each of these, though they do not have an adolescent growth spurt – this is unique to humans. These responses to adverse conditions are vcstcd in genes. These genes confer an adaptive capacity available to any member of the species. The ability of humans to inhabit arctic, savannah, desert and tropical rainforest depends on these adaptive capacities.

It is difficult to sustain the argument that humans who inhabit one part of the world have acquired a particular body size solely as a result of long-term adaptation based on natural selection over many generations. The idea that chronic malnutrition selects against genes that command rapid growth and large body size is too simple, as the experiences of American immigrants show. The smaller body size of people who live in want is the result of responses in growth and development during a lifetime, rather than across many generations. Developmental plasticity has allowed humans to adapt rapidly to changing circumstances brought by migration, famine and war. It has given us an advantage we would not have if we developed along a rigid genetic plan. Responsiveness to the external environment is a tool of human development.

REACHING SEXUAL MATURITY

Whereas in the USA young men and women in affluent families achieve their final heights at around twenty-one years and eighteen years of age respectively, children in communities that are malnourished or exposed to other hardships may continue their growth for longer. Growth can continue until around twenty-five years of age, allowing more time for those whose growth has been slowed to catch up. In the European armies of the nineteenth century the young officers were much taller than new recruits. They had grown up in more affluent circumstances. Through their early twenties, however, the soldiers caught up: they were still growing while the officers' growth had ceased. For growth to continue the maturation of the skeleton has to be delayed, for once the skeleton is mature, growth is no longer possible. Skeletal maturation is linked to sexual maturation.

Rates of growth do not correspond to rates of development. It is usually beneficial for a female to delay reproduction until she is fully grown because her offspring are more likely to survive. If, however, young females are under threat from food shortage or predators, early sexual maturation, before growth is complete, reduces the risk of death before reproduction. There are therefore trade-offs between growth rates and the timing of sexual maturation.

Humans mature sexually before their growth is complete. Maturation of the ovaries and testicles coincide with the adolescent growth spurt. This enables greater adult size than would be achieved by continuation of the slow rate of childhood growth, but has the disadvantage that, when an adolescent girl becomes pregnant, mother and baby may compete for resources for growth – a common occurrence in Asia.

The timing of sexual maturation responds to the conditions of an individual's life. Girls working in factories in Britain in 1830 delayed menstruation until they were, on average, sixteen years old. Over the past century the age of onset of menstruation among Swedish girls fell from fifteen to thirteen years. In Finnish girls it fell from seventeen to thirteen. More food, better living conditions permitted both more rapid growth and earlier sexual maturation. The delayed onset of sexual maturation in European girls in the past allowed them to continue to grow for a longer period, for once a girl has menstruated her growth is almost complete. The average girl grows only about 6 cm (2 inches) after menarche (the onset of menstruation). It is an irony that better living conditions in Europe have lengthened life but shortened childhood. Though many Indian girls are badly nourished and live in poor conditions, they begin to menstruate at around fourteen years of age. To delay maturity until growth is complete may not be the best strategy for them, for the risks of death are high. The disadvantages of the mother and baby having to compete for food to sustain their growth seem to be outweighed by the risk of death before reproduction.

A group of young girls living in orphanages in India were adopted by Swedish families and went to live in Sweden. On arrival they were thin and stunted, but their growth began to compensate and their weights and heights increased rapidly. But, for reasons that are little understood, rapid compensatory growth induced early sexual maturation. Aged around ten, some of the girls began to menstruate. As a group they began at an average age of eleven and a half years, well before the Swedish girls among whom they lived. After puberty their skeletons rapidly matured and growth ceased. They ended up little taller than the girls left behind in the orphanages.

STABILITY AT LAST

Cessation of growth and attainment of maturity bring with them stability in the internal environment. This stability, 'homeostasis', brings with it resistance to harmful influences in the external environment. The resistance, of course, is not total as infections remain dangerous, though much less so than in childhood. While the body grows and develops it is sensitive to the external environment and readily changed by it, but in adult life it becomes resistant. It is therefore appropriate that the search for the environmental causes of heart disease is now focusing on the period of development.

In old age the body again becomes vulnerable to environmental stress. In contrast to the orderly and predictable course of development, the body's decline is disorderly and unpredictable. It becomes less able to use food to maintain itself and less able to repair damage. The orderly course of human development is the product of our evolution, but natural selection may have had less influence on the way the body declines and dies after reproduction has ceased and the genes have passed on to the next generation.

HORMONAL MESSENGERS

Growth involves the division of cells and their expansion, and the accumulation of substances between cells such as the minerals in bone. The proliferation of cells has to be finely controlled so that the final number of cells in each organ is adequate to meet the demands imposed both by other organs within the body and by the external environment. Growth depends on adequate nutrition but also on hormones, which co-ordinate growth in different parts of the body. Chapter 2 described how the constancy of the internal environment is maintained by a central control mechanism in the brain, by the hormonal signals it sends out and by receptors in cells which receive the signals and are set at different levels of sensitivity in different tissues. The same system of hormonal signals and varying sensitivity of tissues to the signals controls growth and allows different parts of the body to grow at different times.

Hitherto food has commanded the rate of growth. Now the rate of growth commands the need for food.

Insulin regulates growth before birth and continues to do so until some point around one year of age when a new messenger, so-called 'growth hormone' acting in concert with insulin-like hormones, takes over. This heralds the second of three phases of human growth. The first, infancy, is a continuation of foetal growth, the second is childhood and the third pubertal. At puberty the sex hormones – testosterone and oestrogen – take on an important role in regulating growth. A feature of body size is that, like blood cholesterol and blood pressure, it 'tracks' through childhood (Chapter 2). Tall children tend to remain taller than other children, while short children remain shorter. At some point in early childhood growth rates become homeostatically 'set' by the internal environment, regulated by growth hormone and less sensitive to the day-to-day supply of food. Hitherto food has commanded the rate of growth. Now the rate of growth commands the need for food. Excess food will not lead to more growth, but to fatness. Observations in animals suggest that appetite is established in early childhood. Every parent knows that children's appetites vary but that any particular child's appetite tends to be relatively constant. Some children are 'good eaters', others are 'picky'. The external environment still influences growth rates in childhood, but the child's initial response to adversity is to maintain its growth, to stay in its track. Girls are better at doing this than boys, a phenomenon seen in other mammals. Ultimately, in both sexes, if adversity persists and is severe, the hormones respond and growth is slowed down.

Because childhood growth is controlled by hormones whose release is controlled by the brain, it becomes possible to understand how psychological stress may impair growth despite adequate nutrition. Elsie Widdowson, the British nutritionist, showed that among German children who were orphaned during the war, those placed in an orphanage with a harsh punitive regime put on less weight than those in an orphanage with a gentler regime, despite having an identical diet. While the scientific evidence on this whole issue remains unclear, few mothers would quarrel with the idea that happy children grow better, and doctors are familiar with the link between bereavement and slowing of growth.

DOWNSTREAM

A difficulty in understanding differences in body size between one child and another is that events at one point in time can have 'downstream' effects, which exert an effect many years later. When, in Indonesia, a group of pregnant women were given extra food, their babies were no larger at birth than those of women not given it. After birth, however, the children grew faster and were taller at five years of age, despite receiving no additional food. Body size at birth has a powerful effect on later growth. In animals food restriction in early development for even a short period may permanently reduce body size. Even identical twins, having identical genes, often have different birthweights. Though this disparity in body size is reduced after birth, it may not be eliminated. In the USA girls who grow up in less affluent homes tend to have less muscle and bone but more fat. Examination of a national sample of babies showed that this was already evident at birth but became increasingly evident up to the age of seven. We do not know whether this amplification after birth is a consequence of childhood living conditions or whether it was entrained in the womb, predetermined by poor muscle development or by persisting changes in the sensitivity of the tissues to hormones.

Because these downstream effects exist it may be impossible to understand how the growth of an individual infant responds to poor food, illness or poor living conditions unless we know its path of growth in the womb. Nevertheless we know the answer to the first of the three questions posed early in this chapter. Infants fail to thrive when the environment is hostile. They expend much of their energy on growth and if they do not consume enough food – and weaning is an especially dangerous period – or if they have to divert energy to combat illness, their growth will falter. Infant growth is controlled by hormones that are sensitive to nutrition.

The second question posed in this chapter is why children who were small at birth or became small in infancy put on weight rapidly in childhood. After one year the speed of growth slows as the child expends less of its energy on growth, which becomes controlled by new hormones less sensitive to nutrition. Body size relative to other children becomes held in a track as though the body had set itself a target. If, however, a child was small as a baby or infant, it may jump the tracks and stage 'compensatory growth'. Why does compensatory growth occur and why does it lead to disease? These are the second and third questions.

GROWTH HAS COSTS

Through natural selection and developmental plasticity living things seek to maximise their reproductive success. This requires them to survive and to have many offspring. Body size is closely linked to reproductive success. Among mammals large males usually have disproportionately high rates of reproductive success while small males may not breed at all. Of the Hertfordshire men who weighed 5½ pounds (2.5 kg) or less at birth 20 per cent did not marry, compared with only 5 per cent of men weighing 7¾ pounds (3.5 kg) or more (Chapter 3). Though large body size may be advantageous, it does not follow that individuals should grow as fast as they possibly can. To begin with there is another way of becoming large: elephants grow slowly but they are born large and grow for a long while. There are necessarily 'costs', trade-offs attached to fast growth. If energy is allocated to rapid growth, the allocation to other activities must be reduced.

Most living things are capable of growing much faster than they actually do. People who fish in rivers become aware of the wide variation in the size of fish according to local conditions. In the streams that flow into Lake Windermere in northern England, brown trout never weigh more than 2 ounces (50g). In the lake itself they can be a hundred times larger, reaching 11 pounds (5 kg). If rapid growth has costs, why do the trout in the lake grow so large? The broad answer must be that the costs are worth paying. If small size makes an animal more vulnerable to predators, or if it needs to reach a certain body size in order to survive the winter or migrate, the ability to grow rapidly and become large will be advantageous.

It is a common observation that after a child's growth has slowed because of illness it will, on recovery, 'catch up' and return to its track of growth. The ability to mount 'compensatory growth' is a common feature in all animals. Farmers are familiar with it: they know that after an inclement season young animals that have been undernourished recover and reach normal mature heights and weights. This may be an essential capacity in animals which, in their wild state, are often subjected to periods of near starvation. The increased growth rate of animals when they are refed is linked to a large increase in appetite which may persist after body size has been restored.

The ability of humans to mount compensatory growth may have originated in the narrow birth canal which developed when humans began to walk on two legs. It became necessary for the two pubic bones to join at the front, to give stability to the pelvis. The cost was a birth canal bounded by bone, incapable of distension. When rickets was common, and many infant girls had softened pelvic bones which deformed when they walked, the costs were high. Many babies died trapped in the deformed birth canal. Even if the canal is not deformed, it imposes limits on how large a baby can grow in the womb. The ability of the necessarily small human baby to catch up, and thereby reduce its risk of death, may be one of the reasons we have acquired or retained this capacity during our evolution.

Slowing of growth during the infant or childhood phases of growth can lead to immediate compensatory growth if adequate nutrition is restored. If shortage of food persists, compensation may be delayed until adolescence. After the importation of slaves from Africa was abolished in 1807, all slaves transported by sea from one port in the USA to another had to have their names, ages, sex and heights recorded on the ship's manifest. Fifty thousand such records have recently been analysed. The slave children were stunted in comparison with modern children. At around fifteen years of age, however, they began to grow rapidly so that they even exceeded the average height of Americans today. This rapid growth coincided with their being better fed, because they had reached an age when they were able to do physical work. Girls had more marked compensatory growth than the boys, and it seems a feature of human growth that during adversity girls hold to their tracks of growth more doggedly than boys and are more resolute in returning to them.

The answer to the second question posed in this chapter is that if a period of undernutrition in the womb and after birth is followed by better nutrition, sufficient to sustain rapid weight gain, compensatory growth will occur. Rapid weight gain may not be accompanied by equally rapid gain in height because after the age of around one year height growth has become tracked under hormonal control.

DIFFERENT BODIES

Although young undernourished animals can restore their body weights by compensatory growth, the composition of their bodies and size of their organs will not be the same as if they had not been undernourished. The balance between the amount of muscle and fat will be different. This is important in the meat industry and much is known about this in farm animals. By contrast, little is known in humans. Experiments with piglets and lambs have shown that organ size can be readily manipulated by different feeding regimes. Three groups of pigs were fed in different ways but all ended up with the same body weight. The weights of their livers, however, were markedly different. Animals that had been well fed early on and then undernourished had smaller livers than those who had been moderately fed throughout, who in turn had smaller livers than the animals that had been undernourished early on and then well fed. The large livers of the last group reflect the continuing plasticity of the liver after other organs are complete and no longer plastic. The early undernutrition of this last group of piglets will have permanently reduced the size of a range of organs, including the kidney, and larger liver size cannot compensate for this. Again, little is known in humans, though studies carried out almost a century ago showed that people in India, Africa and Europe, whose paths of childhood growth are very different, are different in the relative sizes of their organs. Though this may be of only passing interest to anthropologists, it could prove important to the themes of this book.

IMMEDIATE COSTS

In animals rapid growth has a surprising range of costs, some of which are immediate while others are deferred. This has been little studied in humans. Slow growth reduces the requirement for food and allows longer intervals between feeding, but it also enables the nutrients to be used more efficiently. Rapid growth may reduce the quality of the body's tissues. The time required to grow bone is one of the factors that constrain the speed of growth. Specialised bone cells, osteoblasts, make a fibrous scaffolding in which are deposited the calcium phosphate crystals that make the bone hard. This 'mineralisation' of each new piece of bone takes around ten days. Some birds, young cranes for example, need to make a lot of bone because they have long legs. One species, the Sand Hill Crane, is endangered and a group of them were taken to the Wildlife Research Center in Florida. No one really knew what an ideal diet was for a young crane and so they were fed generously with a high-protein diet. They grew rapidly, but suddenly, around three weeks after hatching, their legs began to twist and bend, and the joints in their legs dislocated. Tests showed that there seemed to be adequate amounts of calcium and phosphorous in their diets, and examination of the bones did not suggest that they had suffered from any disease.

Instead it seemed that they had been overfed: the bones had grown faster than the crystals could form, so that they were weakened. The Sand Hill Crane belongs to an assortment of animals, which include horses, poultry and Great Danes, that have the capacity to grow fast but reduce the quality of their bones in doing so. Many elderly people fracture their hips, spines or wrists because they suffer from osteoporosis – thin bones. Current ideas about the causes of osteoporosis are centred on adult lifestyles – smoking, lack of exercise, poor diet. But, as with coronary heart disease, the idea that thin bones are retribution for bad habits leaves much about the disorder unexplained. Studies in Helsinki and elsewhere have shown that elderly people who fracture their hips grew differently from other people as children. Research into the developmental origins of osteoporosis is still at its beginning, but the experiences of the Sand Hill Crane are a central theme. If, in childhood, bones grow at a rate that is too fast to allow proper mineralisation, the loss of minerals that comes with old age will bring weak bones, fracture and disability.

Rapid growth not only weakens bone through poor mineralisation, but may alter its mechanical properties in other ways. Weakened bones are more likely to deform if they have to bear heavy weights. Modern farm animals reach enormous weights, which put a strain on their bones. In pigs this may cause the upper end of the thigh bone to deform at the hip joint. When pigs grow fast under the artificial conditions of modern farming, the growth of the legs is unable to keep up with the growth of the trunk and as a result the hind legs especially are subject to an excessive mechanical load. This leads to deformity around the hip – which may be relevant to humans in whom hip fractures are the most serious complication of osteoporosis.

Difficulties in combining rapid growth and a strong skeleton are shared by many animals. Snails make a skeleton that surrounds them rather than being within them. Periwinkles, *Littorina Littarea,* are abundant on the shores of New England. Their shape differs widely: some are round while others are conical and there are all shapes in between. Inevitably this has been dismissed as genetic variation, the result of natural selection; but a closer look shows that the conical snails live in places that are crowded with many periwinkles, while the round ones live more solitarily. Like other animals, it takes time for a snail to make a skeleton because there is a fixed rate at which calcium salts, in this case calcium carbonate, can be deposited. In less crowded places there is more food and each snail grows faster. Given that the speed at which a shell can be made to cover the body is limited, a round shell is made because it allows more body to be accommodated than a conical one. The cost of a round shell, however, is that it is thinner and the snail is more vulnerable to the dog whelks, starfish and crabs which prey on it.

When an animal diverts energy for purposes such as rapid growth, the symmetry of its body may be sacrificed. Some parts of the body are naturally asymmetrical – the human heart, for example, is on the left, while male fiddler crabs have two claws, a small one for eating with and a large one for waving rhythmically at female fiddler crabs during courtship. Much of the body's function, however, depends on symmetry: legs of the same length, wings of the same size. Symmetry may also be important for the selection of mates. Beautiful human faces tend to be symmetrical. Among male birds who have exaggerated plumage for use in courtship rituals, the females seem to prefer more symmetrical plumage. Symmetry may have importance beyond the choice of mates. Symmetrical, hence more attractive, juveniles may get more food from their parents. More attractive adults may have better social relations with other adults.

A biologist once asked, 'Why are mice the size they are?' There seems no mechanical reason why they should not be larger. Becoming larger must therefore have costs. Though larger mice will tend to have more offspring, perhaps they are more likely to fall prey to the many animals for whom a mouse is food. This can now be put to the test because by genetic engineering 'super mice' can be produced. They make a hundred times more growth hormone than their brothers and sisters, grow twice as fast and become twice as large. But they sleep for twice as long and avoid activity, even grooming of their fur. The energy they have to allocate to growth leads to a crisis, with insufficient energy remaining for movement and normal behaviour. Though this speculation is unsupported by any evidence, it is irresistible to relate some of the languid behaviour of the tall young men in Britain today to the super-mouse phenomenon.

The last few pages have mostly described animals because the immediate costs of compensatory growth have been little studied in humans. The experience of the orphaned Indian girls provides a dramatic demonstration that compensatory growth in children is attended by profound disturbances in physiology. It was hoped that the better food and care they received in Sweden would make them into taller, sturdier adults. Instead, they matured sexually at such a young age that some families thought they must be diseased. There seemed no biological gain from this; instead, they completed growth early and ended up no taller than they would otherwise have been.

DEFERRED COSTS

Some of the costs of compensatory growth are deferred. Direct evidence of deferred costs related to heart disease in humans comes from the Helsinki studies . Men in the studies who lived in less affluent circumstances had more heart disease. That is a common finding in Europe and the USA: the heart disease map of England and Wales, with its red and green areas, was the starting point of our research. Chapter 4 also described how this effect of poor living conditions in adult life was most evident in men who had had low birthweight and were thin at birth, but had rapid weight gain thereafter. They were vulnerable to whatever harmful influences coexist with poor living conditions. Other men were resilient and for them, living in less affluent circumstances had no effect on their risk of heart disease. Other studies described in Chapter 4 show that raised blood pressure and diabetes are also linked to rapid weight gain in childhood, following small size at birth. This may put an excess load on the kidneys, leading to high blood pressure, and an excess load on the pancreas, which makes insulin, leading to diabetes.

As yet we know little about the deferred costs of rapid weight gain in humans. The life of the salmon opens up interesting possibilities. Salmon develop blockages in the arteries of their heart walls, the coronary arteries, which are similar to those that cause heart disease and death in humans. These blockages accumulate slowly as the young salmon grow in the rivers in which they were born. Once the fish reach the sea, the numbers and severity of the blockages increase rapidly. Up until the time of sexual maturity the number of blockages increases progressively as the salmon grows. By the time the salmon are sexually mature, at around four years of age, 95 per cent of them have blockages.

The explanation seems to lie in the change of diet once they reach the sea. While young salmon are in their nursery streams they live largely on proteins in aquatic insects and grow slowly. Once at sea they eat fish, rich in fat, and grow faster. Something connected to rapid growth makes the blockages in their arteries increase. The obvious suspect is the hormones that control growth responding to the high-fat diet. Towards the end of summer the hormone production of fish that are in the river but destined to reach the sea next spring changes. More thyroid and growth hormone is produced. As the animal approaches sexual maturation, testosterone increases. Do the hormones that promote rapid growth also promote the thickening of the walls of the coronary arteries and narrowing of the channel through it? Or does the stress of migration raise the fish's blood pressure and thereby injure the coronary arteries? We do not know. But the story of the salmon, the poor diet in the rivers followed by the high-fat diet at sea, resonates remarkably with the story of the person who develops heart disease, the poor diet in the womb followed by the high-fat diet after birth.

We do not know to what extent the salmon's rapid growth shortens its lifespan. Other animals provide evidence on this. The fast-growing lizards in the meadows of Brittany lead shorter lives than the slow-growing lizards in the mountains of southern France. The caterpillars of speckled wood butterflies living in Madeira grow slowly, because the butterflies can reproduce all the year round, so there is no haste to grow large, become a pupa and emerge as an adult. But speckled wood butterflies in England can only reproduce in the summer. The caterpillars need to grow fast. Caterpillars in Sweden grow even faster and they lead even shorter lives. Allocating more resources to growth reduces the allocation to functions such as maintenance and repair of the body, and hence reduces lifespan.

This can be shown experimentally. Rats that were under-nourished in the womb and remained undernourished after they were born lived for longer than those who were undernourished in the womb but given a better diet after birth. The lives of the latter were shortened by the human equivalent of twenty years. High food intake and rapid compensatory growth lead to a short life, while low intake and slow growth prolong life.

To achieve rapid growth the lizard trades off longevity; many fish do the same. The periwinkles of New England trade off their ability to defend themselves against predators. Poultry breeders are familiar with the trade-off between rapid growth, which is profitable, and reduced immune defences against infection, which increases the risk of death. The growth of living things is not maximised, encouraged to proceed with all possible speed until some mechanical constraint is reached and they can grow no faster. Rather, growth is optimised, limited so that benefits such as larger body size or earlier reproduction are not outweighed by costs, either immediate or deferred.

OPTIMISING HUMAN GROWTH

Heart disease and diabetes are preceded by small size at birth, poor growth during infancy and rapid weight gain thereafter. This is a common occurrence in Western countries, especially among poorer people. The contribution of growth after birth to the totality of these major diseases is not an issue that requires detailed discussion here. It has a large effect and there are plenty of reasons why promoting infant growth and preventing rapid weight gain are important goals for every child. The ways to achieve this are set out in nationally agreed guidelines for infant feeding, weaning and childhood diets. The guidelines are there but, for whatever reasons, they are widely ignored. The next chapter describes how they can be applied to any child.

9

Weaning

During infancy, the first year after birth, and for up to around the first two years of age, growth is sensitive to the environment. It has been known for more than a century that poor living conditions, overcrowding in particular, slow an infant's growth. One reason for this is that overcrowding leads to infective illnesses and the infant has to divert energy and nutrients to combat them. However, like the baby in the womb, an infant's growth ultimately depends on the supply of food. So what, in this brief but highly impressionable stage of a life, should the mother provide?

BREASTFEEDING

Humans are mammals, differentiated from other vertebrates by the way they nourish their young after birth. The tadpole is abandoned in a mass of nutrient jelly after the mother has completed her investment in her offspring and takes her leave. The bird invests in the egg and thereafter does no more than sit on it. After hatching it has another chance to nourish its young, but the system is a clumsy one. The parents leave their young for long periods, days even, exposing them to predators and other dangers. The foal, however, is able to reattach itself to its mother immediately after birth: the breast replaces the placenta.

Bear cubs show that this reattachment can happen without the mother's bidding. Bears, whether brown, black or polar, mate in the spring. The embryo's growth is then suspended through the summer until autumn, when it implants in the womb and begins to develop. Almost immediately the mother ceases to feed and enters a den where she spends the winter hibernating, without food or water. While she sleeps the cubs are born and begin breastfeeding. She awakes to greet her suckling children.

HUMAN BREASTFEEDING

There is no debate that breastfeeding provides ideal nourishment for the human baby, and that the act of suckling helps develop the psychological bonding between mother and baby. Breast milk provides sufficient energy, nutrients and fluid for at least the first four months. Not only does it contain the appropriate balance and concentration of nutrients, but it offers them in a digestible form and contains enzymes to assist with digestion. It also contains a repertoire of cells, antibodies, hormones and growth factors. The antibodies in breast milk combat infections in the baby's gut and are most important in the first month or so after birth. Hormones and growth factors promote the growth and development of the baby's intestines. In the longer term breast-feeding has been linked to lower rates of childhood obesity and better mental development. Even a few weeks of breastfeeding have been shown to confer lasting benefits on the baby.

If it is so widely agreed that breastfeeding is the best way to nourish a newborn baby, why is it that in some Western countries only a minority of babies are fed this way? In the United Kingdom only around 40 per cent of babies are breastfed at six weeks. Historically some areas, such as Scotland, have had much lower rates and rates varied sixfold between different areas of the same city. Mothers' poor nutrition may have made it difficult to provide adequate feeding: crèches and facilities for breastfeeding were often not available in factories, cotton mills and other places that employed young women; or culture and custom may have discouraged breastfeeding. In coal-mining areas, for example, the wishes of men employed in dangerous and demanding jobs may have taken precedence and breastfeeding was perceived as con-flicting with the sexual role of the breasts. But this perception is part of other, older cultures. Mende women in Sierra Leone soon take their infants off the breast and give them tinned milk instead. They, and other peoples in West Africa, believe that a man's semen contaminates breast milk and may make the infant sick. Sexual intercourse cannot be resumed until breastfeeding ceases and early resumption is important to the mother because it helps bond her with the father, on whom she is economically dependent. Today, in many countries, the need for improved workplace facilities for breastfeeding mothers remains an issue. Sweden has demonstrated that changes in attitude to breastfeeding in the workplace and across society can lead to huge increases in breastfeeding – from 20 per cent among two-month-old babies in 1973 to 85 per cent twenty years later.

SUCCESSFUL BREASTFEEDING

Although breastfeeding is successfully accomplished by all mammals, early problems in establishing it may discourage women. Generally agreed practices which help to initiate successful breastfeeding include allowing mothers to feed their babies within half an hour of birth, and not giving the newborn baby any food or drink other than breast milk unless medically indicated. Young women today may know little about breastfeeding. Traditionally, a girl would see her mother, aunts or cousins feeding their babies and learn about it. Today, some young women are repelled by the notion of breastfeeding. In Britain the majority of mothers having their first baby ask for advice on breastfeeding technique after discharge from hospital, and find the help they receive from midwives and health visitors useful. In the early weeks a mother is fatigued from childbirth and is having disturbed nights. Continuation of breastfeeding may depend on the encouragement and physical support given to the mother. If her partner or family does the household chores during this critical period she is more likely to negotiate it successfully.

BOTTLE FEEDING

Some mothers wish to breastfeed but are unable to do so. Happily, although the healthy baby fed exclusively on breast milk for the first four to six months remains 'the gold standard', a mother who chooses to bottle feed can purchase 'infant formulas' with considerable confidence – at least in countries where there is effective legislation. Whereas cow's milk is unsuitable for young infants because it places too great a burden on their kidneys, modern formulas, in which the content of the milk has been modified, provide satisfactory substitutes for human milk. In Europe infant formulas are required, by law, to satisfy the nutritional needs of babies while not providing an excess of any nutrient. The protein in them must come from cow's milk or soya protein. Given that many elderly people alive in Europe today were fed on condensed milk – this was common in the northern industrial towns of Britain, for example – or on other wholly unsuitable substitutes for breast milk, this marks a real advance in the protection of babies. Some mothers have difficulty in preparing a feed from powdered milk accurately and need initial help. Although they are sometimes shown how to prepare a bottle feed during antenatal classes, this is seen as unsatisfactory, if only because mothers who have already decided to bottle feed their babies are less likely to attend these classes. This argues for close individual instruction in bottle feeding after the baby is born.

Scientific understanding of the components of breast milk is incomplete. Formulas will probably never match the remarkable properties of human milk. They are, however, being improved all the time: they allow the mother freedom to work outside the home and enable the care of her child to be shared with other people.

LEARNING HOW TO HANDLE CHOLESTEROL

A question to which much thought has been given in biology, but almost none in medical research, is whether the unique composition of breast milk, its nutrients, hormones and high contents of cholesterol and saturated fat, teaches the baby new metabolic activities which, once learnt, are continued for life. Does the high cholesterol content of human milk – a content far beyond any-thing that has ever been recommended for children or adults – set the way the baby handles cholesterol throughout its life? Does it establish within the baby's internal environment the rate at which its liver makes cholesterol and the rate at which it breaks it down? Is the amount of cholesterol in your blood a marker of the diet you received at this critical stage of your life, when your need for energy – having been met by carbohydrate and protein brought to you by the placenta – became, within a few hours, dependent on a high-cholesterol, high-fat diet? Chapter 2 described how, from around the age of six months, the amount of cholesterol in the blood tends to 'track'. Children with the highest levels early on still have the highest levels ten years later. In animals there is unequivocal evidence that interference with cholesterol metabolism during development changes the way the body handles cholesterol permanently.

Babies need fat and cholesterol

A mother's immediate response to this might be to attempt to restrict the amount of cholesterol she gives her baby. That, however, is counter to a central theme of this book. The baby does not simply depend on the mother for its physical needs, it learns from her. This learning begins in the womb and continues after it is born. The food that it receives may inform its meta-bolism for life. The rich supply of cholesterol in its mother's milk may be instructive, and may teach the baby how to establish a cholesterol system that is adequate to meet the demands of growth and the production of hormones. Hitherto we have assumed that a given cholesterol concentration in the blood is associated with a given risk of heart disease, but a high serum cholesterol at the age of fifty has different components: one is the amount of saturated fat in the food eaten in the past few months, another is the body's competence at handling cholesterol, which in animals is known to be learnt around the time of birth; another is the genes acquired at conception. A particular cholesterol concentration in the blood could have different consequences for health depending on what underlies it.

THE BABY PREPARES FOR WEANING

Both the length and weight of a baby increase rapidly in the first months after birth, and it grows fatter. Most babies double their birthweight in the first five months. This is usual: no one knows if it is optimal. Thereafter, as part of the slowing of growth which characterises human childhood, growth rates fall so that by one year the birthweight has trebled. By the age of six months, fat contributes a quarter of the body weight. After this age there is a **Babies double their birthweight in the first five months** gradual decline in fatness and proportionately more lean tissue – muscle – is deposited. The fat laid down in the first six months provides an important store of energy for the infant to use during weaning, as at this time eating behaviour may be unreliable. There are increased demands for energy when the infant becomes more mobile and when, no longer protected by the mother's antibodies, it encounters common infections.

WHEN TO WEAN?

Standard recommendations are that a baby can thrive on milk alone for the first four months after birth. During this time the gut is maturing and solid foods are not properly digested. In the last fifty years opinion about when to introduce solid food has changed. In the 1950s and 1960s introduction of solids as early as six weeks was **Milk is sufficient for the first four months** popular. This, for reasons that will be discussed, is no longer recommended. At that time cereal mixes were used and commercial 'weaning' foods were becoming increasingly available. (Weaning is defined as the process of expanding the diet to include foods and drinks other than breast milk, or infant formula.)

At some point in the infant's life the volume of milk – breast or formula – that is needed to meet its increasing demands becomes so great that it may be beyond an infant's capacity to drink it and exclusive milk feeding ceases to provide adequate energy. The point at which this occurs will depend on the infant's size and speed of growth, and will therefore differ between one baby and another, and between babies in Westernised countries and in the Third World. The World Health Organisation currently advocates six months' exclusive breastfeeding in both the developed and the developing world, but in the USA and Europe babies fed on infant formula tend to be weaned earlier than those who are breastfed. These variations in weaning practice to an extent reflect different biological needs, as formula fed babies seem to need more energy and are fatter than breastfed babies.

Foods other than milk may be hazardous before the age of four months

In the mid-1970s there were concerns that early introduction of solids might be hazardous, leading, for example, to obesity. Introduction of solid foods before four months was discouraged, but mothers have paid little heed to this advice and many babies in Britain receive some solid food before they reach this age. Family advice, a wish to have the baby sleep all night and a desire to see it progressing to the next stage of development may all lead mothers to begin weaning before four months. This is unnecessary, as milk is an adequate food until around six months, and it may be inappropriate. Babies are born with a 'spitting out' reflex that persists for several months, and the ability to move food around the mouth and chew does not readily develop before three to four months. Young infants do not digest solid food well and their kidneys may not be mature enough to handle the extra load on them which solid food imposes. Where there is a history of asthma or eczema in the family, mothers are encouraged to breastfeed for six months and weaning under the age of four months is particularly discouraged because it predisposes the infant to develop eczema.

CULTURAL DIFFERENCES

In Nepal, women of the Tamang caste travel extensively up and down mountains to cultivate their crops and herd their animals. They are often away from home and have no alternative but to feed their infants on breast milk. Infants are fed whenever their demands coincide with the mother's ability to stop work temporarily and breastfeeding continues for three years. The Tamang women have little choice other than to do this, as the alternative would be starvation. One answer to the question of what, for the baby's nutrition, is the optimal period of breastfeeding, is that it depends on the alternatives, and those are often culturally determined. Across India mothers have a wide range of weaning strategies to match their varying circumstances. In rural areas breastfeeding may be continued for two years, while office workers in the cities may discontinue before six months. While, during weaning, the Western infant can learn to enjoy a diversity of food offered at several meals a day, for many infants in the world weaning is a harsh experience: in the towns of Tigrai, Ethiopia, half the infants receive only one meal of bread or porridge a day. Few ever eat fruit or vegetables.

People have attempted to remove this cultural element and determine what the optimal period of breastfeeding should be if only physiological factors are taken into account. They use monkeys and apes as their point of reference, and conclude that breastfeeding should be continued up to six years of age, though not, of course, as the exclusive source of food. In the English countryside during the Second World War, my wife knew of a five-year-old boy who was still being breastfed: it seems he was conforming with the behaviour of our humanoid ancestors.

In humans and other mammals weaning may bring conflict between the interests of the mother and the interests of the infants. Across the world in many modern-day communities, mothers who work outside the home have to give up breastfeeding early and change their infants to bottle feeding as their work benefits the family, whose interests are part of the equation that determines the infant's period of suckling. Age at weaning on to solid food is the result of a negotiation between each individual mother and her infant. It takes into account the biological needs of the mother, the infant and the rest of the family, and their wishes, whether cultural or individual. Inevitably, to echo a theme of this book, there will be trade-offs. Age at weaning is determined by a balance of interests, which may compete. There can be no prescriptive advice. What is the best age depends on the alternatives. What is right for one family is not for another. And what is best for one baby may not be best for another because each baby is different.

'WEANING NEGOTIATIONS'

The weaning negotiations between the blue whale, the largest of mammals, and its calf involve hundreds of litres of milk. While being nursed the calf consumes more than 350 litres (77 gallons) of milk each day. It puts on 8 pounds (3.6 kg) in weight every hour. The whales breed in the winter in tropical or temperate waters and travel to polar waters to feed during the summer months, journeying in pairs but communicating with other whales through deep, rumbling sounds that are felt rather than heard. During the journey the calf cannot survive without the mother, but once the feeding grounds are reached the negotiation can begin. Having attained about 23 tons (23,400 kg) in weight and 52 feet (16 metres) in length after seven or eight months of suckling, mother and calf part company, and the calf wanders off to fend for itself.

The weaning time of the blue whale is mainly determined by the pattern of its migrations through the oceans. For other sea mammals local circumstances are more important. Stellar sea lions living off the Californian coast seldom suckle their young for more than a year before casting them off. To the north, in the harsher conditions of Alaska, they suckle them for two years. The age at weaning of bottlenose dolphins ranges from three to eight years. So there can be no fixed age at weaning, appropriate to all members of a species. It depends on circumstances – which echoes another theme of this book. Some animals may anticipate weaning by conceiving their babies at particular times of the year. Most African bats conceive and give birth before the insects on which they feed are abundant, and the completion of six weeks of suckling coincides with the ending of the rains and increasing abundance of insects. It takes the infant bats several weeks to learn how to catch and handle food efficiently, but through the mothers' forethought they do this at the time when there is most food available. In the European countryside in the past, the frolicking at harvest time when food is plentiful led to babies that were born in summer, but had to be weaned in mid-winter, when solid food was scarce.

PROLONGED BREASTFEEDING

In Hertfordshire, a group of mothers continued to give their children breast milk beyond the age of one year, though we do not know what other foods they gave them. These mothers tended to be in the poorer families and they prolonged breastfeeding beyond one year as a form of contraception. When they were adults, their sons had higher cholesterol concentrations in their blood than other men and higher death rates from coronary heart disease. Studies in baboons suggest that continued exposure to the thyroid hormone in mother's milk leads the infant to reduce its own production of the thyroid hormone – a response that persists and raises blood cholesterol levels in later life. By Western standards, the poorer women in Hertfordshire were exposing their children to breast milk for an unusually long period, which at first sight might seem an example of the mother asserting her priorities over those of the baby, the conflict between the two that is part of normal biology. It could be argued, however, that they were preventing the arrival of another baby, which would threaten the one already born by diverting the mother's attention and possibly reducing the availability of food.

WHICH FOODS TO USE?

Babies are usually ready to start on solid foods between the ages of four and six months, progressing over the weeks from puréed food to solids that they can pick up with their fingers. Teeth erupt from around six months onwards, and sucking is replaced by biting and chewing. These feeding skills are learnt and pave the way for the successful introduction of solid foods. When a thousand British mothers were asked their views on the choice of weaning foods, 95 per cent considered a wide variety to be important for the baby. Disturbingly, over 80 per cent thought that high-fibre, low-fat diets were also important. Although this view of an ideal infant diet was not always translated into corresponding action, it is a stark illustration of how traditional dietary practices have been distorted by single-issue enthusiasts, whether it is the 'healthy eating' lobby extolling 'fibre is good' or the 'anti-lobby' saying 'butter kills'.

Babies should not have a low-fat diet

FIRST WEANING FOODS

Many different foods can be used during weaning, but at first they must be semi-fluid and soft because the baby has no teeth and cannot chew. Rusks and a porridge-type food based on rice are common first weaning foods. Non-wheat cereals, fruit, vegetables and potatoes are also used. Puréed fruit and vegetables should not be the sole first weaning foods because they contain too little energy and fat. Mothers in Spain use puréed vegetables but add olive oil to increase their fat content. Addition of vegetable fats in this way may be helpful for infants who are being weaned on to puréed vegetables. Infants under six

Rusks, rice and purées

months are preferably not given wheat because it contains a protein, gluten, that is linked to a lifelong disorder of the bowel called coeliac disease and too early exposure to it is thought to increase the risk of the disease.

FOLLOW-ON FORMULAS

Breast milk is a poor source of iron, and solid foods such as meat, bread and pulses allow the infant to meet its needs for iron, which can no longer be satisfied by the stores it received from its mother before birth. At birth the baby of a well-nourished mother has sufficient iron stores to carry it through the first six months, but babies that have been exclusively breastfed commonly begin the second six months with low iron stores. These may lead to anaemia, a common occurrence in the poorer areas of even affluent Western countries. For infants being bottle fed, 'follow-on' formula milks are used to replace infant formulas after six months. Follow-on formula milks are enriched with iron and are not recommended before six months.

Iron is needed after six months

At the outset of weaning, foods should be introduced gradually over the weeks, simply as an addition to the infant's milk intake. Weaning is an opportunity to offer the baby a wide variety of foods, and introduce it to the range of textures and tastes that will form its diet through life. Gradually other foods largely replace milk so that by one year solid food that babies can pick up with their fingers comprises most of the diet and the infant can join in family meals – though some families prefer to feed their infants separately at a quiet time when the child can receive undivided attention. Either way it is important that the infant is supervised during mealtimes: the risk of choking persists through infancy. By two years or before, the diet is similar to that of the rest of the family.

Gradually introduce a wide variety of food

WHAT DO BABIES EAT?

In a recent study of six-month-old babies in Britain, a nurse visited the home and interviewed the mother or the principal carer. The mother was asked about how the baby had been fed since birth and the previous day's food was recorded in detail. The thousands of babies in the study were from families with a wide range of incomes, homes, ethnic backgrounds and lifestyles. The generosity of the mothers who helped with this study gave us a picture of how babies today are being fed and weaned. The names of the babies have been changed.

WEANING TOO QUICKLY

Jordan was 7½ pounds (3.4 kg) at birth. He was never breastfed, but was fed on formula milk for the first five months, after which he was given cows' milk. This is the diary that his mother recorded.

6.25 a.m.		9 fl oz low-sugar squash
7 a.m.	Dried baby muesli mixed with water	
10.30 a.m.	Baby rusk	
12.15 p.m.	Dried rice and vegetable baby food mixed with water	9 fl oz low-sugar squash
3 p.m.	Dried baby dessert mixed with water	
5.30 p.m.	Baby rusk	
6.45 p.m.		4 fl oz cows' milk diluted with 4 fl oz water

For a six-month-old baby low-sugar squash and diluted cows' milk provide insufficient energy. In effect ,Jordan has been completely weaned off milk at the age of six months. This is too early and he continues to need formula milk (follow-on formula). The reason for weaning is that, as the baby grows, exclusive milk feeding does not provide enough energy. For some months after weaning begins the baby requires energy from both food and milk, though ultimately, of course, it will rely on the energy from food alone.

Anna is another baby in the study. She was 7 pounds (3.2 kg) at birth, but is the same size as Jordan (18 pounds – 8.2 kg) and already has many adult foods in her diet, while continuing to drink large amounts of formula milk.

6.30 a.m.	Small pot fromage frais	7 fl oz formula milk
10.15 a.m.	1/2 slice of toast	7 fl oz formula milk
11.15 a.m.	1/2 shortbread biscuit	2 fl oz boiled water
3.15 p.m.	Mashed baked beans and potato	7 fl oz formula milk
7.30 p.m.	1/2 mashed banana	7 fl oz formula milk

As Anna gets older it is necessary for her to progress from puréed food to more solid meals. She is, however, being given toast and biscuits which, as she has no teeth, she cannot chew. There must be uncertainty whether she derives much nourishment from the food, both because she cannot chew it and because she may not be able to digest it at this young age. In contrast the mashed baked beans, potato and banana are appropriate. Like Jordan, she is being 'fast-tracked' through the weaning process, but in a different way.

No chewing food before teeth erupt

After six months, the texture of the food needs to change gradually so that the child learns to chew better. Puréed and mashed food is replaced by whole food. Chewing improves the co-ordination of the mouth and tongue, which is important for the development of speech.

Babies need a variety of textures

SHOULD I USE BABY FOODS?

Ben is an only child. He was not breastfed, but was fed from birth on one formula milk. At four months of age, he began to eat some solid foods, beginning with a dried baby dessert reconstituted with water.

8 a.m.	Jar of creamed porridge	5 fl oz formula milk
12 noon	Jar of broccoli and potato bake	5 fl oz formula milk
4 p.m.	Jar of apricot custard	5 fl oz formula milk
7 p.m.		7 fl oz formula milk
10.30 p.m.		8 fl oz formula milk

Ben was 7 pounds (3.2 kg) at birth and now weighs 19½ pounds (8.8 kg). He is therefore putting on weight satisfactorily, having more than doubled his birthweight by six months of age. He is being fed exclusively on jars of baby foods and formula milk. His diet lacks variety of texture and could be expensive.

Compare it with Stephen's.

2.30 a.m.		8 fl oz formula milk
9 a.m.	Baby rice mixed with formula milk	7 fl oz formula milk
12 noon	Puréed courgette, potato with melted cheese	5 fl oz formula milk
4.30 p.m.	Mashed banana	8 fl oz formula milk
Midnight		8 fl oz formula milk

Stephen was 8½ pounds (3.9 kg) at birth, but is now smaller than Ben, weighing 17½ pounds (7.9 kg), and still at an early stage of the weaning process, taking small amounts of solid food. Stephen's mother gave up breastfeeding after ten weeks 'because he was irritable and there was not enough milk to satisfy him'. He was given formula milk and two weeks later received his first solid food, baby rice – one of the commonest first weaning foods in Britain.

Follow-on formulas replace formula milk at six months

At five months his milk feed was changed to a 'follow-on' formula containing iron. This change to follow-on formula was a little earlier than the recommended six months. He is now being given a range of foods prepared at home and either mashed or puréed. Some parents find it convenient to use foods already prepared as 'baby dinners' or 'baby foods'. These are a useful adjunct to the family's meals, but not a substitute. Baby foods are designed to contribute to the immediate needs of a

Baby foods are not a substitute for family food

brief phase of life – weaning. From one to another they vary greatly in their nutrient content, and they are expensive. Sharing family meals introduces the baby to the varied and balanced diet which he or she will enjoy for a lifetime.

AFTER SIX MONTHS

After six months new foods, including meat, fish, eggs, all cereals and pulses, can be introduced. These are already part of family meals, cooked at home, and can readily be puréed or, as the baby gets older, mashed or minced, or at a later age chopped. It is no less time-consuming to prepare small rather than large amounts of baby foods, which can be frozen for later use. The recommendation is that cows' milk should not be the main milk drink before one year of age.

It is important that foods containing iron – meat, fish, dark-green vegetables, bread and pulses (peas, beans, lentils) – form part of the weaning diet. Meat, pulses and wholewheat products are also important sources of zinc, a nutrient essential for child growth that is found in lesser amounts in refined cereal products.

Zinc has a vital role in the growth and differentiation of cells, as children who are deficient in it fail to grow. It may be necessary for the signalling systems by which the body controls its responses to growth hormone. There is a strong lobby that advocates supplementing the diets of pregnant women in poor countries with zinc. Though it may seem an attractive option, the 'magic bullet' approach to improving the health of pregnant women and their children in the developing world has many opponents. A recent study in Bangladesh showed that zinc supplementation led to poor mental development. Foods containing iron and zinc should

Foods containing iron and zinc are necessary

be part of the varied, balanced diet to which an infant is gradually introduced at weaning. Iron in meat and fish is more easily absorbed than iron contained in cereals and pulses. However, iron absorption from these latter foods is helped by vitamin C consumed in the same meal, good sources of which are fruit and vegetables.

TWO GOOD WEANING DIETS

Harry was exclusively breastfed for four months, after which he received additional formula milk and began to eat baby rice. He was 9 pounds (4.1 kg) at birth and is growing well, now weighing 21 pound (9.5 kg) at the age of six months. He eats an extremely varied diet based on puréed family foods, which are served as meals. This, together with the follow-on formula milk introduced at six months, will protect him from iron deficiency and consequent anaemia. His mother continues to breastfeed him.

5 a.m.		20 min breastfeed
7.30 a.m.	1/2 Weetabix, cow's milk and boiled water 3/4 mashed banana	
8.30 a.m.		10 min breastfeed

10.15 a.m.		10 min breastfeed
1 p.m.	Puréed chicken, tomato, onion, mushroom, potato Pot fromage frais Stewed mango	
2 p.m.		2 min breastfeed
4 p.m.		10 min breastfeed
5 p.m.	Mashed swede, potato, butternut squash, parsnip Mashed pear	
6.30 p.m.		6 oz bottle formula milk

Emily was 6½ pounds (2.9 kg) at birth, and is also enjoying a varied diet. She is the second of two children. She was breastfed for seven weeks, after which her mother returned to work as a clerk in an office, leaving Emily in the care of her grandmother during the day. During the week before the day of the diary, she had eaten a wide range of food – chicken, potatoes, other vegetables, bananas, stewed fruit and baby rusks.

7 a.m.		7 fl oz formula milk
11 a.m.	Puréed potato, carrot, parsnip, broccoli Stewed apple and pear	4 fl oz formula milk
3 p.m.	Baby rusk	4 fl oz formula milk
5 p.m.	Small pot fromage frais	3 fl oz baby juice
7 p.m.		7 fl oz formula milk
8.30 p.m.		1 fl oz formula milk

VITAMIN SUPPLEMENTS

Current recommendations are that from the age of six months infants receiving breast milk as their main drink should be given supplements of vitamins A and D. Infants fed on formula milks do not need vitamin supplements, provided their consumption of infant formula, or follow-on formula milk is more than one pint (500 ml) per day. If they are consuming infant formula or follow-on milk in smaller amounts, or they are being given cows' milk, vitamins A and D supplements should be given. As already noted, cow's milk is not recommended as the main milk drink before the age of one year.

INDEPENDENCE

Biology demands that the child is set free from its dependence on the mother and weaning is part of this journey. It carries the infant from dependence on a high-fat diet, provided by milk, to a varied adult diet in which most of the energy is supplied by carbohydrates. Weaning requires the infant to learn to enjoy new foods. A food that is initially rejected is often readily accepted after repeated experiences. There is preliminary evidence that breastfed babies are better able to adjust to new foods because the mother's milk has a range of flavours and odours that is lacking from formula milks. When your infant refuses food, spits it out, tips it over, puts its hand in it or throws it on the floor, be reassured that you are taking part in a universal experience. Infants quickly learn to try to get their own way and may reject savoury foods if they know that a sweet food, which they usually prefer, will eventually be given. Weaning requires time and encouragement, and success may come sooner if solid foods are offered from a spoon or given as finger foods. The infant needs to learn how to handle food in order to diversify its diet. After six months, as sucking is replaced by sipping and swallowing, the infant can begin to feed from a cup. Bottle feeding is generally discouraged after the age of twelve months.

The infant's introduction to the wide variety of tastes and textures of foods on which it will live for the rest of its life is a critical phase of its development. The pre-school child should be enjoying a diverse diet that contains items from all of the five food groups described in Chapter 6. It is a common observation that weaning behaviour, with a child getting its own way, rejecting savoury foods in favour of sweet foods, refusing to explore new foods, may continue through early childhood. It is as though the weaning negotiations that should have ceased at the age of one are still in progress. Persistence of weaning behaviour long after weaning has ceased has varying manifestations. A child may successfully manipulate its own diet so that only pizza and burgers are offered. The child's continuing desire for fatty foods, possibly a legacy of its happy experiences of milk, may lead it, after victory over the mother, to a diet of fatty and sugary foods. The baby's natural liking for sweet food (and breast milk is remarkably sweet) may persist and transform into demands for sweets and confectionery. The reluctance of a baby to abandon milk and experiment with other foods may lead to a childhood diet which is limited in variety and clings to familiar and readily palatable foods.

Weaning behaviour may persist into childhood

Although we do not know to what extent the tastes and preferences acquired during weaning continue to influence dietary choices throughout life, common sense suggests that the infant that learns to enjoy a wide range of different foods will be more likely to continue with a diverse and varied diet.

FOUNDATIONS OF A VARIED AND BALANCED DIET

Sophie (birthweight 8 pounds – 3.6 kg) enjoys her food. She was breastfed for nearly six months, when her mother felt that 'it was the right time to stop'. She is now drinking follow-on formula milk. Sophie tasted her first solid food – baby rice – at four and a half months. In the week before the day of her diary she had eaten a variety of dried baby foods and family food – meat, potatoes, pasta, vegetables, yoghurt and fruit.

7.30 a.m.	2 baby rusks	4 fl oz formula milk
11 a.m.		5 fl oz formula milk
1 p.m.	Dried chicken and vegetable baby meal mixed with water Mashed broccoli Dried baby dessert mixed with water	2 fl oz baby juice
4 p.m.		5 fl oz formula milk
5.30 p.m.	Homemade spaghetti bolognaise Mashed banana	2 fl oz boiled water
8 p.m.		6 fl oz formula milk

She is laying the foundation for the varied and balanced diet that will promote her own health through life and the well-being of her children in the womb. The study of British children shows that mothers successfully wean their children in a wide variety of ways. There are a number of recommendations and one or two rules. Don't introduce solids too early; don't give puréed fruit and vegetables as the only first weaning food; after six months give follow-on formula and iron-rich foods. But mostly weaning is a negotiation to be enjoyed by both partners. Unlike the blue whale, who abandons her child at a time when it can become wholly independent, the dialogue between the human mother and her baby is protracted and at the end of it the child is still not independent of the mother. It is a theme of this book that millions of years of evolution have primed the baby and mother to achieve a successful outcome. For our forebears and for many women in the world today, the choices of weaning foods are limited. Today Western mothers have new choices – dried baby foods, fortified foods, organic foods, baby food in jars and cans. They can buy their toddlers food shaped like animals or letters of the alphabet, food with toys, cartoon characters made from pasta, teddy bears made from crisps. But these are diversions – the core of successful weaning remains unchanged. Over a period food gradually replaces milk so that by one year it comprises most of the diet. Though the infants may initially resist, they have an instinct to experiment with an increasing variety of food of different textures and tastes. Biologically they cannot remain for ever dependent on the mother and must set themselves free. For many babies weaning is preceded by separation, the cessation of breastfeeding, a private dialogue between mother and baby. The journey from dependence on milk to dependence on solid food may be a negotiation with the whole family and its success may depend on many people – father, brothers, sisters, grandparents, childminders.

AFTER WEANING

Finally the child reaches the fourth phase of its changing relationship with its mother. In the womb it lives off her body and what goes into her mouth. After birth it lives off breast milk, then it lives off weaning food and finally it lives off family food. By around the age of two a new trajectory of growth has been established. It is controlled by growth hormone, which takes over the regulation of growth from insulin, which has controlled growth more or less since conception. Beyond two years of age, feeding your child more food than it needs will not promote its growth. It will not become an Olympic high jumper if you give him or her extra food, it will merely become fat. Food does not command growth. Rather, growth and physical activity command the amount of food a child requires.

The child probably needs three meals a day, with a couple of snacks such as a banana, a piece of bread, taken from the foods within a balanced diet. Children, at least until the age of two, require the fat and vitamins in full-fat dairy products. Skimmed milk is not suitable for children under five years. The publicity given to the possible danger of excess animal fat for older

Children under two need fat

children and adults has led to a widespread misconception that fat is bad for babies. It is not. National recommendations for the diets of adults have no relevance for children under two years, for whom the provision of sufficient fat is a priority.

CHILDHOOD GROWTH

Children who are born small and thin but gain weight rapidly are at increased risk of heart disease and diabetes in later life. When these findings were first published they gave rise to understandable concern. When babies are born small, it is a universal practice to encourage weight gain during infancy, the first year after birth. Did these new findings suggest that this increases their risk of having a heart attack in later life? They did not. Gain in weight and height between birth and the end of infancy at one year of age reduces the risk of heart disease and diabetes in later life. We do not know precisely why this is, but it is similar in principle to growth before the baby was born. Greater growth is associated with better function of systems such as that which regulates the amount of sugar in the blood, and larger size of key organs such as the liver. During infancy two organs – the brain and the liver – remain plastic. Good growth seems to be linked to better function of these organs, reflected in greater intelligence in later childhood and better handling of cholesterol. Only after the age of one does rapid weight gain begin to have damaging effects.

A child's relative height is expressed as 'centiles', which range from 1, the shortest children, to 100, the tallest. A child of average height is therefore on the fiftieth centile. A child's growth 'tracks' along centile lines: small children tend to stay small in relation to other children; large children tend to remain large. If their growth falters at any age after birth, their centile position moves downwards to a line of lower value. Because growth may falter if a child is unwell, or becomes undernourished, or stressed, crossing centile lines downwards serves as a warning that the child is not thriving. Simply because a child is tall it does not follow that it is thriving. He or she needs to be maintaining their centile position. Children who fail to thrive tend to become thin before their growth in height slows. They therefore cross centile lines for weight before crossing those for height. In some children who fail to thrive, a clinical illness is discovered. In others, the cause may be feeding problems or psychological difficulties. A child that is undernourished because of feeding or behavioural problems may show no signs of being hungry or be eager to feed when food is offered. Children who consume snacks and large volumes of diluted sweetened juices frequently have poor appetites for more nutritious foods. One of the important functions of child welfare clinics is to monitor the centile positions of the children at repeated visits.

Falling 'centiles' of weight and height are a warning

Centile lines are not the same for all populations. Because of the differences in growth rates between boys and girls – differences which are now thought to underlie some of the higher rates of heart disease in men – there are separate charts for boys and girls.

A child's fatness is measured by its weight in relation to its height, usually expressed as its body mass index. Chart 4 on page 182 allows a child's body mass index to be calculated from its height and weight – in the same way a woman's body mass index was calculated on page 130. Body mass index is correlated to fatness: a higher index indicates a fatter child, although it is not a direct measure of fat. For example, a child may have a high body mass index because it is exceptionally muscular. The waist circumference provides an additional check because fat children generally have large waists. Charts 2 and 3 on pages 178 and 179 show the centile lines for body mass index in the United Kingdom, and the internationally agreed levels of body mass index above which a child is either overweight or obese. The charts show that body

A child's body mass index measures its fatness

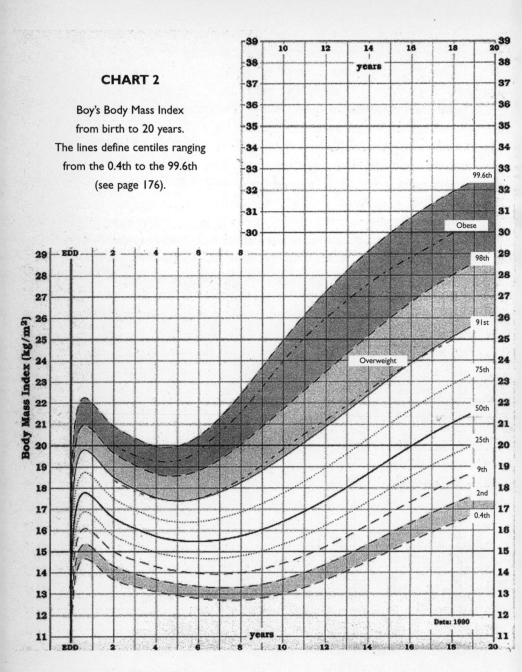

CHART 2

Boy's Body Mass Index
from birth to 20 years.
The lines define centiles ranging
from the 0.4th to the 99.6th
(see page 176).

Body Mass Index (kg/m²)

99.6th

Obese

98th

91st

Overweight

75th

50th

25th

9th

2nd

0.4th

Data: 1990

years

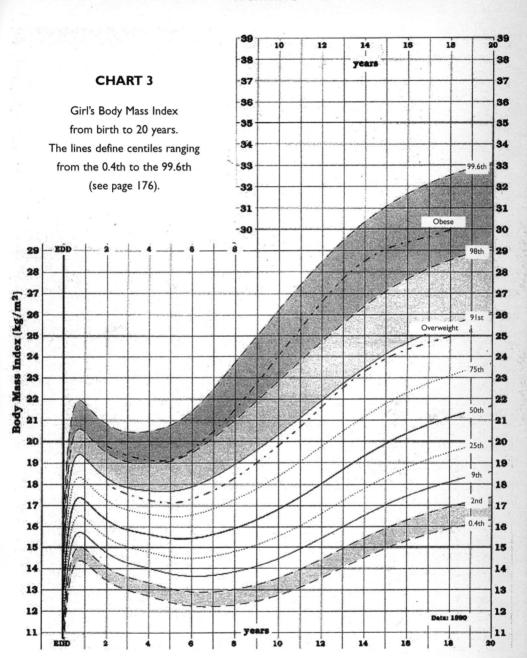

CHART 3

Girl's Body Mass Index
from birth to 20 years.
The lines define centiles ranging
from the 0.4th to the 99.6th
(see page 176).

mass index changes as children grow older. Between birth and one year babies get fatter and their body mass indices rise sharply. After that age, as the child grows taller, but does not continue to require large fat stores, the body mass index falls.

THE ADIPOSITY REBOUND

At around six years of age the body mass index begins to rise again, the so-called 'adiposity rebound'. The timing of this rebound is critically important to the later development of obesity and diabetes. Inspection of Charts 2 and 3 shows that among children who were thinnest at the age of twenty, the body mass index did not rebound until around eight years, whereas among the children who were fattest the rebound occurred at around four years. Adiposity rebound at an early age is now known to predict obesity in adult life. It gives us a new way of monitoring the fatness of our children and can help identify those who will become obese long before they do. This is especially important because the increasing fatness of children in Western countries, and in developing countries that are rapidly becoming affluent, is a source of great concern. It is not simply that a rising minority of children are becoming obese and unable to take part in normal physical recreations. More and more children are attaining levels of overweight which were previously unknown. I have a clear recollection of the precise number of overweight boys and girls with whom I went to school in England during the Second World War. There were none. This is a recent and rapidly rising epidemic.

THE OBESITY EPIDEMIC

In the past decade it seemed a reasonable policy to try to lower the levels of fatness by altering the diets and patterns of physical activity of all schoolchildren. Attempts to do this on a large scale have been extremely disappointing. The strategy is also flawed conceptually. We know from studies in which children have been followed up from infancy over many years that there are different childhood pathways to adult obesity and they begin before school age. Most fat infants do not stay fat in childhood; but by the age of around eight or nine years, after the adiposity rebound, the pattern of fatness through adolescence and into adult life is largely set.

Until very recently if twenty physicians such as myself had been asked to identify which in a group of two-year-old children were destined to develop diabetes in later life, we would have pointed to the fatter ones. We would have been wrong. Though there is a general tendency for fat two-year-olds to become fat adults, we now know that the road to diabetes begins with thinness, at birth, in infancy and at two and three years of age. This is followed by an early adiposity rebound and accelerated weight gain. An early adiposity rebound, occurring between three and six years of age is, for reasons we do not understand, more often triggered in thin children, not fat ones. Children having an early adiposity rebound are not the fattest children in the nursery class, but they are those gaining weight most rapidly. Modifying the quotation by D'Arcy Thompson in the last chapter, 'To say that children of a given age vary in the rate at which they are putting on fat would seem to be a more fundamental statement than that they vary in the fatness they have attained.' Though the children who later develop diabetes are not the fattest children in the nursery class, their early adiposity rebound will lead them to being among the fattest children by the age of around eight years.

MONITORING YOUR CHILD'S FATNESS

These new findings point to the importance of monitoring the change in body mass index of a young child and trying to prevent an early adiposity rebound. Young children who are already fat are not the ones at greatest risk of later chronic disease, but they are at risk of remaining overweight. Fatness, however, is undesirable for many other reasons including limited mobility

CHART 4: BODY MASS INDEX CALCULATOR FOR CHILDREN OVER 3 YEARS OLD

Height in feet & inches	Weight in stones																Height in cm
	1.5	2	2.5	3	3.5	4	4.5	5	5.5	6	6.5	7	7.5	8	8.5	9	
2'11"	12	16	20	24	28	32	36	40	44	48	52	56	60	64	68	72	89
2'12"	11	15	19	23	27	30	34	38	42	46	49	53	57	61	65	68	91
3'1"	11	14	18	22	25	29	32	36	40	43	47	50	54	58	61	65	94
3'2"	10	14	17	20	24	27	31	34	37	41	44	48	51	55	58	61	97
3'3"	10	13	16	19	23	26	29	32	36	39	42	45	49	52	55	58	99
3'4"	9	12	15	18	22	25	28	31	34	37	40	43	46	49	52	55	102
3'5"	9	12	15	18	20	23	26	29	32	35	38	41	44	47	50	53	104
3'6"	8	11	14	17	20	22	25	28	31	33	36	39	42	45	47	50	107
3'7"	8	11	13	16	19	21	24	27	29	32	35	37	40	43	45	48	109
3'8"	8	10	13	15	18	20	23	25	28	31	33	36	38	41	43	46	112
3'9"	7	10	12	15	17	19	22	24	27	29	32	34	36	39	41	44	114
3'10"	7	9	12	14	16	19	21	23	26	28	30	33	35	37	40	42	117
3'11"	7	9	11	13	16	18	20	22	25	27	29	31	33	36	38	40	119
3'12"	6	9	11	13	15	17	19	21	23	26	28	30	32	34	36	38	122
4'1"	6	8	10	12	14	16	18	20	23	25	27	29	31	33	35	37	124
4'2"	6	8	10	12	14	16	18	20	22	24	26	28	30	31	33	35	127
4'3"	6	8	9	11	13	15	17	19	21	23	25	26	28	30	32	34	130
4'4"	5	7	9	11	13	15	16	18	20	22	24	25	27	29	31	33	132
4'5"	5	7	9	11	12	15	16	17	19	21	23	25	27	28	30	32	135
4'6"	5	7	8	10	12	14	15	16	18	20	22	24	25	27	29	30	137
4'7"	5	7	8	10	12	13	15	16	18	20	21	23	25	27	28	29	140
4'8"	5	6	8	10	11	13	14	16	17	19	20	22	24	26	27	28	142
4'9"	5	6	8	9	11	12	14	15	17	18	20	21	23	25	26	27	145
4'10"	4	6	7	9	10	12	13	15	16	18	19	20	22	24	25	26	147
4'11"	4	6	7	9	10	11	13	14	16	17	18	20	21	23	24	25	150
4'12"	4	6	7	8	10	11	12	14	15	16	18	19	21	22	23	25	152
5'1"	4	5	7	8	9	11	12	13	15	16	17	19	20	21	23	24	155
5'2"	4	5	6	8	9	10	12	13	14	15	17	18	19	20	22	23	157
5'3"	4	5	6	7	9	10	11	12	14	15	16	17	19	20	21	22	160
	10	13	16	19	22	25	29	32	35	38	41	44	48	51	54	57	
	Weight in kilograms																

and psychological problems. It is those who are gaining fat rapidly between the ages of two and six years of age, crossing centiles of body mass index upwards, who are at the greatest risk of both diabetes and heart disease – though diabetes is much more strongly related to fatness than heart disease. We therefore need to monitor a child's tempo of fat gain as well as determining whether at **After three years increasing fatness may be dangerous** any particular age a child has a body mass index above some threshold level which defines overweight. As with height, it is not the size at any particular age that is the main focus of concern, but the change – in the case of height it is the falling centiles – over an interval of time. It is therefore appropriate to regularly record the height and weight of children up to school age and beyond.

PREVENTING AN EARLY ADIPOSITY REBOUND

So if a child's body mass index begins to increase at four or five years of age, what can you do? Although the precise causes of the epidemic of childhood obesity are widely debated, and the role of hormones such as insulin and growth hormone remains to be defined, two culprits are universally acknowledged – snacking between meals and lack of physical exercise. Production and wide promotion of a completely new range of easily stored, ready-to-eat snacks, often high in sugar and fat, has been a major change in the Western diet over the past twenty years. Snacking while watching television seems to be a common problem. Children and adults with weight problems often have undisciplined eating habits and a good way to overcome this is to adhere to the three meals a day pattern of eating described in previous chapters. Childhood obesity may be a family matter, involving the family's eating habits. If a child becomes hungry between meals, fruit, bread and breakfast cereals are all low in calories. A general recommendation is to correct the patterns of eating and restrict access to the energy-dense foods high in sugar and fat, before reducing portion sizes at meals.

The decline in physical activity among children in Western society is recognised as a major influence in the obesity epidemic. In Britain only 8 per cent of children walk to school. Less exercise reduces the need for energy in food. One of the strongest predictors of childhood obesity is the presence of a television in the child's bedroom. As, increasingly, parents are unwilling to allow their children to walk to school or roam the streets and footpaths, structured physical recreation in schools and clubs becomes the alternative way to maintain adequate levels of physical activity among children.

One of the strongest predictors of childhood obesity is the presence of a television set in the child's bedroom

10

Pathways to Health

Heart disease, stroke, diabetes, hypertension, osteoporosis – the most common causes of human illness and death – seem to originate in two universal phenomena. The first is plasticity during development, each individual's response to the conditions of life. 'This marvellous plasticity, the ability of living things to develop structures and functions that permit them to solve problems imposed by local peculiarities, has been a source of everlasting wonder,' wrote René Dubos. Like Darwin, pondering many years before why animals with the thickest fur came from the coldest climates, he recognised the dual action of genetics and developmental plasticity in meeting the challenges of an ever changing environment. It accords with the general life history theory of living things that undernutrition in the womb and during infancy has long-term costs, which include premature disability and death. We are beginning to understand the biological processes through which this operates, and how they make an individual more vulnerable to influences such as obesity and poor living conditions in later life.

The second phenomenon underlying the diseases which will disable or kill many of us is compensatory growth, the ability to grow rapidly following a period of undernutrition. Few living things grow as fast as they can because the costs of rapid growth are not worth paying. For humans, one cost appears to be chronic disease in later life, but as yet we know little about the biological processes. If it seems implausible, or counter-intuitive, that growth can be harmful, then suspend your intuition. Research into goitre, the deforming enlargement of the thyroid gland that accompanies iodine deficiency, was held up for years because people could not believe that a deficiency caused swelling.

What seems implausible to us often turns out to be the way things are. I cannot believe that every autumn the Arctic Tern leaves the tundra within the Arctic Circle, where it breeds, and flies down to the edge of the Antarctic ice pack where it spends the winter, and flies back to the Arctic the following summer. It flies 21,000 miles each year, roughly the circumference of the earth. It seems unbelievable, but it happens to be true. Before you read this book, did you know that well-intentioned attempts to give impoverished mothers more protein resulted in smaller babies, or that feeding orphan Indian girls with better food distorted their sexual physiology, or that ewes give birth to bigger lambs if they are poorly nourished in mid-pregnancy?

OUT OF TOUCH WITH NATURE

A hundred years ago in the USA and Europe measures were taken to try to prevent so many children from dying. Food, sanitation and hygiene were improved, and it worked. Fewer children died, and they grew faster and larger. Surely larger children must be good, a triumph of public health? But biology now questions this. Why is it good? Are there costs? René Dubos again:

> One of the criteria of health most widely accepted at the present time is that children should grow as large and as fast as possible. But is size such a desirable attribute? Is the bigger child happier? Will he contribute more to man's cultural heritage? Or does his larger size merely mean that he will need a larger motor car, become a larger soldier, and in his turn beget still larger children? The criteria of growth developed for the production of market pigs would hardly be adequate for animals feeding on acorns in the forests and fending for themselves as free individuals. Nor are they for men. Size and weight are not desirable in themselves, and their relation to health and happiness is at most obscure.

Human well-being is fincly balanced. In exchange for a few centimetres' gain in height, we have perturbed the reproductive biology of the next generation. In 1959 an editorial in the *Lancet* remarked that it was becoming difficult to find choirboys. The race to an earlier puberty left too little pre-pubertal life in which musical skills could develop. Such changes happen slowly and we have come to accept them. We still accept small, thin, stunted, newborn babies as part of normal life. A quarter of all babies born in our maternity hospital are thin: we think little of it. Since they are usual, they must be 'normal'. We accept that now that there is more food available, small babies in Western countries and in the cities of the Third World are able to compensate by rapidly putting on weight. It is 'normal' in that it is a biological response that has been passed down to us through our genes from fish. It is becoming usual, but it is leading to heart disease and diabetes. We have created the conditions in which epidemics of these diseases are occurring. We could restore more appropriate conditions if we wished.

Through developmental plasticity we can change our biology by changing nutrition during development. The escape from hunger is a triumph of Western civilisation. Through Acts of Parliament we improved the lot of children; because food is abundant it is less advantageous for them to grow slowly and make only small demands on their families. They grow faster, but at the cost of shorter childhoods. In a shorter childhood the brain may need to develop more rapidly to be able to meet the demands of maturity and independence. We invented the light bulb, and in many countries children can now play, read and learn for more hours than was ever possible before. We invented the television and children became more sedentary.

Though Acts of Parliament and invention may initiate universal changes, their costs, often unpredictable, are borne by each individual. As individuals we need to understand what is happening to our biology and why we have created diseases. Long ago the pathologist, Virchow, wrote, 'Disease is life under changed conditions.' Ordinary people in Western countries have never been in a better position to control their lives, to improve the internal environments of their children and adjust their external environments, their diet and activities, to their internal environments. But they need the information and guidance.

We have lost touch with the natural world. Heart disease appeared in our midst, a new disease. We took refuge in simplistic ideas: too much milk; too many eggs; too many cigarettes. Smoking is a considerable insult to the body and no one I know advocates it. But when the last cigarette has been thrown away, there will still be heart disease and diabetes, and osteoporosis and breast cancer and the other diseases that arise out of changes in our biological systems as we develop.

Chapters 6 and 7 described the principles of a varied and balanced diet for women before and during pregnancy. The recommendations conform to those widely accepted on both sides of the Atlantic. Within the broad guidelines there are many choices, determined by levels of activity, body size and preferences. But people today seek prescription, not choice. 'They' should tell us for how many minutes to exercise each day, how much milk to drink, how many portions of fruit. Pregnancy books give table upon table of how much of each nutrient there is in each food, how many portions are desirable, and there are many charts and diagrams. Armed with a little knowledge, however, there are countless different ways in which a woman can negotiate the dietary needs of pregnancy. If she is already on a varied and balanced diet, why change it?

The quality of the diets of those of our forebears who lived in rich farmlands would not have been greatly enhanced had they had access to modern nutritional knowledge. Science did not make good diets better. The Mediterranean diet was not invented in a laboratory. The triumphs of nutritional science have been in rescuing people from dietary deficiencies created by human society: rickets in the slums of Glasgow, pellagra in the southern states of the USA, protein-calorie deficiency due to poor weaning practices in the Third World. Most Western women have access to rich farmlands – in their local supermarket. Cut off from tradition and lacking the requisite simple knowledge they are not, however, able to make good choices.

In human societies customs take root which fly in the face of nature. The French realised long ago that, needing tall, strong young men for their weakening armies, they had to protect girls and young women – the mothers of the future. Across India, feeding of the boy child is given priority over the feeding of the girl and the young wife is the last to eat. Many young women in Western countries aspire to be thin, and diet and shrink themselves. By contrast, in other animals large size and well-developed sexual characteristics – be it genitalia, plumage or a courtship song – demonstrate fitness. Why do some young Western women wish to show themselves as less fit? Why do others want to pretend to be fitter than they are, having surgery to make large breasts larger still? We need to find a balance.

We have created the junk food industry for our children. The typical American eats three hamburgers and four orders of French fries every week. Never was it easier for a child that was born small, or became small in infancy, to stage compensatory weight gain. Compensatory growth is commanded by an increased appetite; this is satisfied by nutritionally inadequate, but highly palatable, junk food, which generates a continuing appetite – for junk food. Animals in zoos offered choices of food will eat diets that are palatable even though they are nutritionally inadequate. The palatable foods they are offered are not available in the wild.

We are not seeking a return to Arcadia, an imaginary past of sturdy peasants nourished by robust foods. 'They' cannot help. Each family has to make its own food decisions because each family is different.

PATHWAYS TO DISEASE

Darwin recognised that the fittest individuals – those who survive and reproduce – are those best adapted to the external environment. Bernard realised that fitness depends on the interplay between the internal and external environment. The fittest people are those best able to resist the impact of the outside world and maintain constancy within their bodies. The internal environment is established during development, through plastic responses to nutrition and other aspects of the external environment. It modulates our responses to the conditions in which we live. We know that our early experiences of measles, chickenpox or mumps condition our responses to the viruses when we again encounter them – a particular example of a general phenomenon which underlies disease. The men in Helsinki who grew well in the womb are indifferent to poor living conditions, at least insofar as these predispose to heart disease.

Disease does not have a single cause. The tubercle bacillus is required in order for people to develop consumption. Koch's discovery of the bacillus encouraged the idea that for each disease there was a single cause. But in the past the tubercle bacillus was ubiquitous, and who became sick and died, and who met the bacteria's challenge and became for ever resistant to it, was determined by their nutritional state, their internal environment. Now geneticists look for single causes, 'the gene for heart disease'. There is no single gene, there are many and what they do depends on what is happening elsewhere in the body. Genes do one thing in one person and another thing in another.

A well-known entertainer died recently, stricken with a rare disease. His widow wrote that he died 'from an entirely random disease, neither hereditary nor caused by lifestyle'. The essence of most human disease is not about a single overwhelming disruption of the body occurring either at conception or in middle age. There are pathways to disease. It is like a game of pinball: the ball is launched by a spring, it strikes a pin projecting from the surface of the table, it is deflected according to the speed and direction from which it came. The pin's effect on the ball is conditioned by what has gone before – the way the spring launched the ball. The ball moves on until it strikes other pins, which pin it strikes is determined by what has gone before – how it was deflected by the previous pin. Eventually it disappears down a tunnel, having amassed a score, depending on which pins it has struck. Health in a lifetime is launched by the mother and a strong launch goes a long way to ensuring a good score. The well-grown baby becomes vulnerable if it fails to thrive in infancy. But if it thrives it can withstand rapid weight gain and poor living conditions in childhood and adult life, and reach old age in good health. A weak launch, poor growth in the womb, leaves the baby vulnerable, to a degree that may depend on its genes. Low-scoring pins await it – rapid childhood weight gain, poor living conditions. It is not doomed, but it is vulnerable.

FURTHER RESEARCH

As was long ago articulated, but until recently forgotten, the effects of the physical and social environment on our health cannot be understood without knowledge of individual history. Researching the biological and social pathways to heart disease, stroke and diabetes is a new challenge. As the idea emerged that these diseases are essentially disorders of development, it received strong support from three groups of people: the general public, biologists and doctors. For some 'reductionist' scientists who study fragments of the body, cells, molecules and genes, rather than the body's systems, an obstacle to embracing these new ideas has been the lack of understanding of how their particular fragment is linked to human development and hence to later disease. But we are all agreed that there are glaring gaps in our knowledge that research can readily fill. We know little about how the mother's diet and body at the time of conception affect the growth of her baby. We know a lot about it in sheep, pigs, cows and horses, because breeding domestic animals is a major industry. We are beginning to learn about the human baby's responses to undernutrition in the womb and during infancy, but much more research is required. We do not know why compensatory growth leads to human disease, although much is known about this in farm animals.

The public wants more research on these themes in humans. Thousands of them are helping in studies around the world. They are not sick and have little to gain personally. For no financial reward they give their time, submit to intimate measurements and blood tests: some even spend days and nights in hospital. To many of them it is obvious that the best possible start in life is the greatest gift society can give to the next generation.

RETURN TO LANCASHIRE

So what went wrong in Lancashire, creating in the cotton towns one of the epicentres of the heart disease epidemic? This was the life of a textile worker in Manchester in 1832: 'He rose at 5 a.m., worked from 6 to 8, and then returned home for half an hour for breakfast of tea or coffee and a little bread. Work resumed until noon when he had an hour for dinner, the poorer workers dined on potatoes and a little melted lard or a few pieces of fried fat bacon, the better off on potatoes and a small amount of meat. Work then continued until 7 p.m., followed by supper of tea and bread.' His external environment, his diet and activity, were outside his control. His poor living conditions harmonised with those he experienced in the womb and during infancy, but his life expectancy was only fifty years.

When did prosperity arrive in Lancashire and what was the manner of its entrance? Did it sneak in, a bit more meat and a little more sugar and a little less fibre year by year? No. It arrived in 1870 and it made a grand entrance. Throughout the nineteenth century real wages in the Lancashire cotton towns increased only slightly until 1870. Low standards of housing and hygiene persisted. In the early 1870s, however, there was a boom in wages and a mass consumer market began to emerge. The high wage economy in the Lancashire towns was surpassed only by London. At that time half of the income in working-class families was spent on food. Between 1874 and 1894 the price of bread, tea and sugar halved, while cheap meat – mutton, beef – became increasingly available. During the 'cotton famine' of the early 1860s, which was occasioned by the American Civil War and cessation of cotton exports from the Southern states, families had subsisted largely on bread and oatmeal – though interestingly the health of babies improved because their mothers, now unemployed, were able to stay at home and care for them. From the 1870s onwards, everything changed: 'fry-ups', shop-made pies and cakes, fish and chips were available to all – provided their families were employed. Food poured in, from the USA, from Denmark, and elsewhere in Europe. While Lancashire began to feast, the Southern states of the USA slid into chronic malnutrition. This is likely to have effects down several generations (Chapter 5). It will cast a long shadow and it created the stroke belt. Even in Lancashire a substantial group of people – 25 per cent in working-class Manchester – remained in primary poverty, their incomes below the level necessary to sustain physical health. Not until the twentieth century did they have ready access to high-energy foods. The shadow of this is still with us, part of the social inequalities in Britain, the worse health of the poor.

In the early years of the nineteenth century the widespread employment of women in the cotton industry ameliorated the poverty engendered by inadequate wages paid to men. In the later years of the century, when most wives and the vast majority of unmarried women and adolescent girls were employed in the mills, their wages produced the high incomes that allowed families to share in the consumer boom and have access to plentiful high-energy foods. The cost of high family incomes, however, was the poor health of women and their babies.

RETURN TO JOHN CLEGG

So why did John Clegg, the non-smoking slightly overweight truck driver, have a heart attack that evening in Burnley? He was born in the town in 1955. His mother had also been born in the town, between the two World Wars, into the third generation of a family of Burnley cotton workers. She grew up during the Depression. Her home was typical of many in Burnley at the time, overcrowded and difficult to keep clean. Successive government housing acts had removed the worst homes – the poorly ventilated back-to-back houses where so many infants had died. But the town council did not have the money to improve its houses on a large scale. Since everyone in his mother's family over the age of fourteen years was employed, they were not short of food. Her own mother, like herself, had been born in the town but her grandparents had migrated in as children, their families no longer able to earn a living on the land in the north of the county. They had fled the failing cottage industries to join the burgeoning factories in the mill town, where workers were in demand and wages, though meagre, were steady. Her father's family had moved up to Burnley from Liverpool to work in the coal mines; and John's father was a miner.

John was born without mishap after a normal pregnancy, during which his mother continued to work. As his father remarked, he looked a bit 'puny' at birth; he was thin, though, weighing 6½ pounds (3 kg). His grandmother reared him while his mother continued to work, and though he remained skinny as an infant the health visitor who came to the house at intervals was unconcerned. Many infants in Burnley were thin, she said. By this time the family had moved to one of the high-rise flats built by the town council after the war, despite the protests of many local people who wanted to continue living in streets. Though the flat was new and had a bathroom, there was less opportunity for playing outside with other boys. He became fatter, though he was far from being the fattest boy in his class. He lacked the endurance for 'serious sport' beyond casual games of football. When as a young man he was offered a job as a truck driver he was glad to accept.

What could he have done to prevent his heart attack? He was born vulnerable to heart disease, being thin at birth. He put on weight rapidly in childhood, which gave him a high fat mass in relation to his muscle mass. For him, to have maintained a low body mass index was more important than for many of his friends. He may also have been more liable to raise the lipid levels in his blood if he ate fatty foods, or to raise his blood pressure if he ate excess salt, but that, at the moment, is conjecture. Fortunately, his heart attack led to his high blood cholesterol and blood pressure being discovered and he has been taking tablets ever since. The vision for the future is that such abnormalities will be identified soon after birth. He has not been able to return to work. He has lost confidence in his body; fears another heart attack while he is driving, with terrible consequences. He no longer has an evening pint of beer with his friends at the Royal Butterfly. Though grateful for the tablets which keep his cholesterol and blood pressure down, he wishes he had never been ill and were back driving his truck.

THE THIRD WORLD

Because so many children die in Third World countries they have been the focus of attention by international agencies, UNICEF, the World Bank, the World Health Organisation. Increasingly, however, it is becoming apparent that, though the growth of many infants in the Third World is slowed by difficulties at weaning, the origins of the widespread stunting of growth lie in the womb, in the mother. A further cause for concern is that with high-energy food becoming increasingly available, stunted children in the cities of the Third World are starting to become overweight. Why stunted children so readily become overweight is the subject of ongoing research: it could be their low muscle mass or it could be their hormones. But a drive through Mumbai (formerly Bombay) shows that the world epidemics of heart disease and diabetes – the latter will soon affect 200 million people – are being fuelled even in the slums. Studies in the cities and in the countryside tell the same story. The pathway to heart disease and diabetes in India is similar to the pathway in Western countries: small size at birth followed by rapid gain in weight.

In order to promote the nutrition and health of girls and young women so as to improve the growth of babies, another issue has to be confronted. Across most of Asia, including China, and much of North Africa death rates among women are considerably higher than would be expected from the death rates among men. Since, given the same nutrition and health care, women generally have lower death rates than men, this suggests that women are being neglected. It has been estimated that there are around 100 million fewer women in the world than there would be if they were not neglected – 37 million in India, 44 million in China. Three components of this neglect have been identified. First, girls are given less food than boys and are less likely to receive health care if they are sick. Second, young women of reproductive age are thin through undernourishment. As a consequence of this many babies are born with low birthweight: 20 per cent of babies born in south Asia in the year 2000 weighed less than 5½ pounds (2.5 kg). In California babies are considered for intensive care if they weigh less than 6 pounds (2.7 kg), which would apply to more than half of all babies born in India. Finally, in later life women have high rates of disorders known to be the result of malnutrition – recurrent illness and inability to do physical work. Among both men and women death rates from 'cardiovascular disease' – heart disease, stroke and high blood pressure – are higher in south Asia than in any Western country.

The intense concern of doctors and health workers of all kinds in Asia is evident from the flourishing programmes of research there. The first world conference on the 'Foetal Origins of Adult Disease' was not held in the USA or Europe, but in India. International concern is rising, but the agencies grapple with politics. They are necessarily diverted into handling crises such as AIDS and become distracted by taking on issues such as smoking which, though damaging, does not lie at the heart of human well-being.

Underlying the epidemics of heart disease and diabetes that accompany Westernisation is our inability to improve the nourishment of babies in the womb as rapidly as we can improve the nutrition of children. During the so-called 'nutritional transition' children are immediately able to benefit from the increased availability of food, but for the full benefit to reach babies it takes more than one generation, because part of a mother's ability to nourish her baby depends on the size of her body and her nutritional stores, which are the product of her growth and nutrition since infancy, and indeed, of her own foetal experience. Mothers who had low birthweight tend to have babies with low birthweight. During the period of transition many small babies are born but are able to gain weight rapidly in childhood – the pathway to later disease. In a few generations – and animal experiments suggest it may be three – the growth of babies improves and rates of heart disease begin to decline, as has recently occurred across the Western world.

Genevieve Stearns, a nutritionist at the University of Iowa, has summarised the position in the following way:

> The best provision for well-being in any period of life is to arrive at that point in good nutritional and physical status. The well-born infant is sturdier throughout infancy than the baby poorly born; the sturdy infant has stores to give impetus to growth in the pre-school years. The child who is in excellent nutrition will have stores to be drawn upon during the rapid growth of puberty. The well-nourished mother can nourish her fetus well; therefore the best insurance for a healthy infant is a mother who is healthy and well-nourished throughout her entire life, as well as during the period of pregnancy itself.

From this it follows that during the nutritional transition, the nourishment of girls and young women should be the highest priority, as it was in France. Neglecting this in favour of older people or boys and young men sets the stage for the kind of outbreaks that occurred in Lancashire.

RETURN TO MOHAN RAO

Mohan Rao lay in the bed next to John Clegg in Burnley General Hospital. He had diabetes although he was only thirty-five years old. It is a characteristic of the rising epidemics of heart disease and diabetes in India that they affect people at younger ages than is usual in the West. Mohan said that his family came from Mysore, a city in south India, where these diseases are unusually common. Mohan was born in Burnley, but his mother grew up in a village just outside Mysore. Predictably, Mohan weighed only 6 pounds (2.7 kg) at birth, but this caused no concern because the midwife knew that Indian women tended to have small babies. Small babies are the product of scarcity of food in the past and several well-nourished generations will need to pass before its harmful effects on foetal growth can be reversed. It is also the product of the higher priority given to feeding of boys and young men over girls and young women. Mohan's mother was no exception.

Growing up in Burnley, Mohan put on weight rapidly as a child. At the age of thirty-five he was not fat, but Indian people tolerate even modest levels of overweight poorly. One recent study of a group of men and women in India has shown that, at the early age of thirty years, the blood sugar levels of many of them begin to rise steeply. They are becoming diabetic. That is what befell Mohan.

MOTHERS CAN BE CONFIDENT

For so long as the main aim of pregnancy is the avoidance of disaster – a dead or deformed baby – a mother may feel that she will be to blame if something is left out of her diet and things go wrong, but she will not realise that the varied and balanced diet which she is advised to eat will give her baby the best possible start and promote its health for a lifetime. Aware of possible guilt, mothers have taken refuge in the prescriptive pregnancy guides that set out the nutrient content of each food – which vitamins, which minerals, how much of each – and recommend the amount of the food and the size of the portions that should be eaten. In Britain the Department of Health recently announced that five spears of asparagus constituted one portion of vegetables – not four spears or six, but five! We do not use such prescriptions for our children's diets after birth: how many apples, pieces of bread, or slices of meat? We offer variety and balance and recognise that the demands of physical exercise and growth differ from one child to another. Each child develops along a unique path, both before and after birth, and its needs cannot be met by formulas as though it were a machine. The plane that will take me from Southampton to France tomorrow is the product of precise design and an inflexible maintenance routine. It makes the journey twice a day according to a tight timetable. Hundreds of thousands of migratory birds make the same journey each year – prepared by nature, guided by instinct, they fly to a timetable determined by sunshine, wind and weather.

Today, in the Western world a mother can enter pregnancy with confidence. She is the custodian of a marvellous system handed down to her and her baby through millions of years of evolution. Natural selection has honed the system for success. Growth and survival of the baby is a centrepiece of evolutionary strategy. Most of the process is controlled by nature: the egg's journey to the womb, the embryo's implantation, the growth of the placenta, all occur without her knowledge. The long and complex supply line which brings food from the mother to the baby develops without her consent. But her body is the arena for nature's performance and over this she can have control. Through a varied and balanced diet, begun before conception, she can start her baby on a pathway which, continuing with good growth in infancy and avoidance of rapid weight gain in childhood, will lead it to a healthy life. The pathway stretches beyond the life of the child to future generations, who will benefit from the diets of mothers today.

INDEX